SAINT PATRICK'S OF MONTREAL

Saint Patrick's, 1897
Courtesy of Saint Patrick's Basilica.

Saint Patrick's of Montreal

THE BIOGRAPHY OF A BASILICA

Alan Hustak

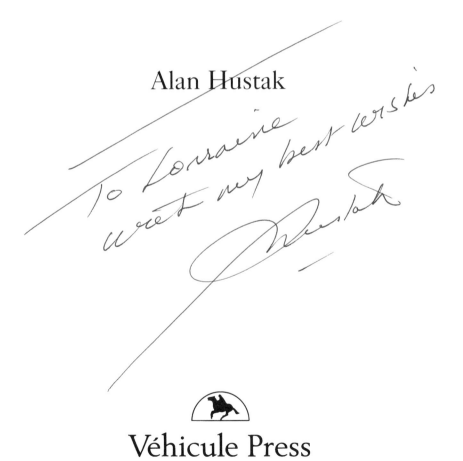

To Lorraine
with my best wishes

[signature]

Véhicule Press

DOSSIER QUÉBEC SERIES

Cover design: J. W. Stewart
Cover imaging: André Jacob
Front cover photograph: P. J. Gordon, June 20, 1905.
Typesetting: Simon Garamond
Printing: AGMV / Marquis Imprimeur Inc.

CANADIAN CATALOGUING IN PUBLICATION DATA

Hustak, Alan, 1944-
Saint Patrick's of Montreal : the biography of a basilica
(Dossier Québec series)
ISBN 1-55065-100-5

1. St. Patrick's Basilica (Montréal, Québec)–History.
1. Title. 11. Series.

BX4605.M6S48 1998   282 .71428   C98-900198-9

Published by Véhicule Press
P.O.B. 125, Place du Parc Station
Montreal, Quebec H2W 2M9

vpress@cam.org

http://www.cam.org/~vpress

Distributed by GDS
30 Lesmill Rd., Don Mills, Ontario M3B 2T6

Printed in Canada on alkaline paper.

A la mémoire de
Gilles Dubois
1942-1991

A church is a diagram of prayer, and the spire a diagram of the highest prayer of all. God chooses you to fill the diagram with glass and iron and stone, since the children of men require a thing to look at.

—William Golding

Contents

Acknowledgements

This is neither an authorised nor an official history of Saint Patrick's Basilica but a highly subjective layman's account of the church in Montreal where I have worshipped off and on, for 30 years. The basilica can be appreciated on its own as an historic landmark, but the experience becomes infinitely richer if a visitor peeks into the storehouse of memory and tradition where its most enduring treasures are to be found. Originally I planned to write a mere pamphlet for the 150th anniversary, but the pastor at the time, Monsignor Russell Breen, thought a book was overdue and suggested something more substantial "if it didn't cost the church anything." He opened the archives to me. His successor, the present administrator, Monsignor Barry Egan-Jones, has been equally supportive. An official history was considered at the time of the church's 75th anniversary in 1922, but the "minute details of the origins of Saint Patrick's and the full exhaustive treatment that will be accorded them in an authoritative history" promised by the wardens was never realised. In fact, no record of such a manuscript, if it was ever written or even begun, could be found. In 1944 a book for the centennial in 1947 was talked about, and "a sum set aside for a scribe with a deft hand and an historical mind who would undertake the task." None was found. I am not sure whether I have a deft hand or an historical mind, but at last a book has been written.

It could not have been done without the generous support of Ted Byfield, publisher of *Alberta Report* who, when others hesitated, instantly recognised the project as "something that's got to be done," and, out of his own pocket, helped fund the research. Simon Dardick at Véhicule Press was similarly enthusiastic. Burdened with more profitable endeavours, he agreed, in spite of its narrow subject matter, to publish the book because "it's a story Montrealers should know about." I am especially indebted to Mary McGovern, the basilica's business manager who patiently put up with my questions and cheerfully helped me raid the vaults to find the answers.

Emmett Cardinal Carter was frank in his recollections. Bishops Leonard Crowley, Neil Willard, and William Power were similarly helpful. Charles Brocklehurst, the late Bruno Harel and his successor, Marc LaCasse, at the Sulpician Archives in Montreal and I. Noye at the Bibliothèque de la Compagnie de Saint-Sulpice in Paris and John Napier Turner were also of assistance, as were the archivists at Concordia University Archives. Joanne Norchet helped translate old documents, and Maureen Hoogenraad at the National Archives of Canada and Sister Raymonde Sylvain, archivist at the Congregation of Notre Dame, unearthed valuable material. I am also grateful to Francis Knowles, Donald Mooney, Rev. Robert Toupin, Edgar Collard, Elizabeth Collard, Paul Waters, Moïra LeBlanc, Sister Gaëtane Chevrier, Eric Durocher at the *Catholic Times* because of his meticulous attention to detail, Conrad Graham at the McCord Museum, Carol McCormick, Luann Wilson Sainsbury at the *Chronicle Journal* in Thunder Bay, Ont., Msgr. George Bourguignon, Margaret Wittich, Albert Biondi, Peggy Curran, Eleanor O'Callaghan, Janice Kennedy, Nick Auf der Maur, Gordon Beck, R. Bruce Henry, Vicki Marcok, and John Mahoney. Appreciation also to *Gazette* librarians Agnes McFarlane, Michael Porritt and Donna McCutchin, and especially to Robert G. Ramsey and Stéphane Lajoie-Plante.

I am not Irish. I am not a theologian, nor am I the church archivist. Although I was taught by Jesuits and describe myself as a practising Roman Catholic, I am far from being proficient at it. Much more practice is required, and I have a long way to go before I get it right.

Any failings in the manuscript, as in life, are mine and mine alone.

A.M.D.G.

Preface

The 150th anniversary of Saint Patrick's Church (now a basilica) is in a sense the celebration of the history of a particular people. The flight from Ireland in the 1840s because of the potato famine was a tragic event which was the root cause for so many Irish immigrating to Canada. This impetus was coupled with the general oppression of the people of Ireland by the British. In the end, what was Ireland's loss became a significant gain for what was known then as the Province of Lower Canada.

This history of Saint Patrick's Church is an important work which not only serves to mark its 150th anniversary, but is an important addition to the history of the Irish in Canada. Through intermarriage with the French-speaking people of Quebec and with peoples of other national groups, the blood of the Irish courses in the veins of many a Canadian.

The clergy and the people of Saint Patrick's are indebted to Alan Hustak for writing the history of the church. This volume will become for many a precious record and a reminder of the Irish in Montreal and their place in the life of the City of Montreal.

Rev. Monsignor Barry Egan-Jones,
Saint Patrick's Basilica

Introduction

A TRUMPET FANFARE resounded through Saint Patrick's Basilica in Montreal on a clear, cold Sunday morning, March 16, 1997, and a capacity crowd of 3,000 in the church rose to its feet as two Roman Catholic Cardinals and seven mitered bishops*, including the pastor of the church, Bishop Leonard Crowley and the Anglican bishop of Montreal Andrew Hutchison, followed two gold processional crosses, thurifers, priests and acolytes in the ritual march down the centre aisle. The processional hymn, "I Will Arise," the words of "Saint Patrick's Breastplate" set to music, was stirring but not exultant. It was after all a time of contrition, the fifth Sunday in Lent. Yet it was obvious this was no ordinary mass. The sanctuary was ablaze with candles, the church decorated with 20 baskets of white gladioli swathed in green ribbons. A red throne erected on the gospel side (left) of the altar signalled the presence of the primate emeritus of Ireland, Cahal Brendan Cardinal Daly. On the epistle side (right) sat Montreal's archbishop, Jean-Claude Cardinal Turcotte. The superior of the Grey Nuns, Aurore Larkin was there. The federal Minister of Finance, Paul Martin, Quebec's Minister of Citizens' Relations and Immigration, André Boisclair, the Mayor of Montreal, Pierre Bourque, and Vera Danyluk, president of the Urban Community's executive committee occupied the front pews. Behind them were Ireland's Minister of Education, Niamh Bhreathnach and the Irish ambassador to Canada, Paul Dempsey. The dignitaries had assembled in prayer to observe an historic milestone in the life of the community and of the church: the Basilica's 150th anniversary.

Cardinal Daly climbed the stairs to a pulpit now reserved for ceremonial occasions. During his homily he described the church as "a truly magnificent building, majestic in its Neo-Gothic splendour, a wonderful monument to

---

*André-Marie Cimichella, Jude Saint-Antoine, André Rivest, William Power, Neil Willard, Leonard Crowley, and Andrew Hutchison.

the fervour and generosity of those poor immigrants from Ireland a century and a half ago, and a tribute to the zeal for God's house and for God's people of the great line of pastors who have served this church and this parish and have so often restored the building and enhanced its original beauty over the years."

This, then, is the story of the church, of its parishioners, and of those pastors "who enhanced its original beauty over the years."

Chapter One

A CHURCH IS BUILT of glass and iron and stone but it takes time and incomprehensible tradition to build a great one. Saint Patrick's Roman Catholic Basilica in Montreal has for 150 years stood foursquare astride a gentle downtown slope known as Beaver Hall Hill. In the 19th century the hill was high ground with a commanding view of the St. Lawrence River, and the church was the focal point for the working-class Irish Catholics who lived in the tumbled slums below: Griffintown, Goose Village and Point St. Charles. Today Saint Patrick's is boxed in by office towers. From the outside it is a massive, strong, almost forbidding place darkened by a century and a half of pollution. Its forecourt—once green and pastoral—has been turned into a parking lot. The basilica's glory is inside, a surprisingly cheerful, vast, uplifting space that author Brian Moore once described as "a brown-and-gold Gothic world of soaring beauty." Virtually every inch of the vaulted interior is embellished. Long, narrow stained-glass windows cast bars of muted amber light across the nave. Veteran newspaper columnist Tim Burke said the effect is "an understated masterpiece of worship. In the majestic silence the struggle of the human spirit seems to rise into a crescendo from time immemorial to eternity." With its pillars, pinnacles, statues, and glowing glass, the interior projects a radiant, sacred presence. The theme of community is written in the detail of its interior design, which is a testimonial to the Communion of the Saints—the union of the faithful on earth with the saints in heaven and the souls in purgatory. The decoration is an instant reminder of St. Augustine of Hippo's belief that all Catholics stand on the shoulders of giants. Or, as one parishioner once put it, at Saint Patrick's "memories of a glorious past come out of the shades and the spirits of great men hover above."

Saint Patrick's has had a parade of distinguished communicants: Louis Riel's Aunt Lucie was married there; the assassinated father of Canadian Confederation D'Arcy McGee was buried from the church; the French-

Canadian poet Émile Nelligan was baptised there; Montreal Mayors Dr. William Hales Hingston, James John Guérin, and James McShane were major boosters; and Canadian Pacific Railway baron, Lord Thomas Shaughnessy an important benefactor. Governor General Georges Vanier's mother, Margaret Maloney, worshipped there as young girl. Toronto's Emmett Cardinal Carter, his brother Alex, a former bishop of Sault Ste. Marie, and the late Gerald Berry, a former Archbishop of Halifax, were altar boys at Saint Patrick's. William Power, the bishop of Antigonish, N.S. sang in its boys' choir. Quebec Premier Maurice Duplessis made it his church in Montreal. Prime Minister John Turner was one of its wardens. Prime Minister Brian Mulroney's youngest son, Nicholas, made his first communion from the church. It is where world figure skating champion and two-time Olympic bronze medalist Isabelle Brasseur married American pairs skater Rocco (Rocky) Marval.

Parent church to Montreal's 250,000 English-speaking Roman Catholics, Saint Patrick's was built between 1843 and 1847 by an association of clerics from France, the Company of Priests of Saint Sulpice. The building that stands is much larger and far more important in stature than the one originally planned. At first the church was to be nothing more than an auxiliary chapel of the existing French-language parish church of Notre Dame on Place d'Armes. Events, however, conspired to bestow Saint Patrick's with more authority and influence than anyone at the time could have envisioned.

According to diocesan records the first Irish Catholics, no more than a dozen of them, came to Quebec in 1710. A few more came with the 99th Irish Regiment which was garrisoned in Montreal after the British conquest in 1759.

The Sulpicians, a syndicate of secular priests with headquarters in Paris, established their first mission in Montreal in 1657 and ten years later were named seigneurs of the island. In theory, they were subservient to the bishop of the diocese of New France, 300 kilometres away in Quebec City. In practice, they zealously guarded their fief. For almost two centuries they looked after Montreal's religious, commercial, and social needs. The Sulpicians were forever doing things without approval from the bishop's palace in Quebec City. In those days Christ's warriors spent as much time doing battle with each other for ecclesiastical jurisdiction as they did fighting for souls. Rivalry between the Sulpicians and the diocese began in 1659 when François de Laval, allied with the Jesuits, was sent from France to become the first bishop of Quebec instead of the obvious choice, Gabriel de Thubière de Lévy de Quills, the superior of the Sulpician mission who was already in Montreal. Mistrust deepened after the British conquest when clerics in Quebec City suspected the Sulpicians of having been co-opted by the enemy. When Montreal surrendered, the British allowed the Sulpicians to retain their seigneurial rights on the island and agreed to compensate them for any property that had been confiscated. The British also strengthened the Sulpicians' hand by suppressing the Jesuits, their only rivals on the island. Relations between the diocese and the Sulpicians were further aggravated when the Sulpicians insisted on referring administrative disputes to the colonial secretary in London rather than to the Holy See in Rome.

Matters didn't improve when the Sulpicians honoured George III's consort, Queen Charlotte, by naming the bell in their Montreal parish church of Notre Dame after her, or when they kicked off the public subscription campaign in 1809 to finance a monument in Place Jacques Cartier to commemorate British Admiral Horatio Nelson's victory over the French fleet at Trafalgar. Civility was suspended in 1819 when the archbishop in Quebec appointed Jean-Jacques Lartigue, a native-born Canadian, as auxiliary bishop responsible for Montreal. Although Lartigue was himself a Sulpician, the company had proposed its own candidate for the position. The Sulpicians did not want Lartigue because they did not think he was qualified and they believed he had been considered only because he was politically well connected. His uncles were prominent Liberal politicians—Louis-Joseph Papineau, Denis Viger, and Benjamin Cherrier, all members of Quebec's House of Assembly who would play a part in the rebellion against British colonial rule 17 years later. When Lartigue was consecrated bishop in 1821 the Sulpicians simply refused to accept him as their superior. They expelled him from their seminary and threw the bishop's throne, or *cathedra*, out of their parish church. Thus humiliated, Lartigue was forced to live at the Hôtel Dieu hospital until 1825 when his own cathedral church of St-Jacques le Majeur at the corner of St. Denis and Ste. Catherine Streets was completed.

The War of 1812 stimulated Montreal's economy and what had been a trickle of immigrants from the United Kingdom grew into a flood. In 1814 Montreal's population was 9,000, 70 percent of it French-speaking; 20 years later the city had a population of 35,000, almost one-third of it Irish. Because of their sheer numbers, English-speaking Roman Catholics were used as convenient pawns in the power struggle between Josephe Vincent Quiblier, the pugnacious superior of the Sulpician Order in Montreal, and his rival, the equally determined archbishop in Quebec City, Bernard Claude Parent.

The schism between the Sulpicians and the diocese deepened in 1831 after Quiblier became superior of the Quebec Sulpicians. He was only 34 and Lartigue refused to accord him the dignity of vicar-general. Five years later, when the diocese of Montreal was established with Lartigue as bishop, Quiblier responded in kind.

A sly man of fierce intellect, Quiblier was born in Colombier, France, June 26, 1796. He studied theology in Lyons and was ordained in Grenoble in 1819. When he arrived in Montreal the number of English-speaking Roman Catholics was so insignificant that the congregation gathered in the tiny sacristy of Notre-Dame de Bonsecours to hear mass. It was said at the time there were so few, "all could be covered by a carpet."

The first wave of Irish immigrants came to escape the persecution of Catholics in Ireland. Under penal laws imposed by the British, Catholics in Ireland could not buy property, vote, hold public office, join the army, carry a weapon, nor own a horse worth more than five pounds. There were no Catholic schools, and mass could not be publicly celebrated. Many of the Irish who could afford to come to Canada worked on building the Lachine Canal in the 1820s. Slowly the number of English-speaking Catholics in the city grew. By 1830 they numbered so many the faithful were moved to St. Helen's, the old Recollect Church at the corner of St. Hélène and Notre Dame Streets, which the Irish promptly dubbed "the Reggilie." It too soon proved to be inadequate. One parishioner, Thomas Hewitt, recalled "seeing the people, Irishmen and women who attended mass on Sundays in the summer season, kneel half-ways out in the street because that church was too small; their attitude and the beads in their hands earnestly told passers-by the zeal that prompted them to hear mass under such disadvantages, for they could neither see the altar nor see nor

Msgr. Josephe Vincent Quiblier, V.G.
From *L'Album du Séminaire de Montréal* (1902)

hear the priest when he preached, but notwithstanding they were praying and waiting for the tinkle of the little bell. They frequently formed the subject of conversations amongst the people at large and many remarks were made on the want of Church accommodation for the Irish, but they were foreigners to Canadians, yet they were Catholics. One priest—(Patrick Phelan*) he was Irish—did all he could for them, but he was bound by ecclesiastical jurisdiction and he had to leave the case to force itself upon those who had the power to remedy their want of a larger church for his countrymen."

The bishop in Quebec City was ambivalent to the spiritual needs of his English-speaking parishioners in Montreal for several reasons. There had never been any English-speaking Catholics of consequence in the diocese before, and in the larger scheme of things there was no need for yet another church in Montreal. There was certainly no shortage of pews: the cathedral Lartigue had built for himself could seat 3,000. The Sulpicians had countered by building their new parish church, the present Notre Dame Basilica which opened on Place d'Armes in 1829. It can accommodate 10,000. All these pews in a city of 20,000, a quarter of it Protestant. Moreover, the liturgy was in Latin, a universal language. The majority of those who identified with the English Catholic congregation, in fact, at home spoke Erse, an Irish form of Gaelic. Because the Irish were Roman Catholics, Quebec's religious leaders assumed they would adopt a natural solidarity and fraternity with their French-speaking brethren. The prevailing attitude among French Canadians as Mavis Gallant has described it so succinctly was: "The Irish were not English. God had sent them to Canada to keep people from marrying Protestants." It was expected they would assimilate. Typical of the sentiment at the time was the letter in the newspaper *La Minerve*: "As strangers, because they are from beyond the seas, should not (the Irish) upon their arrival here accept our usages and customs and conform to them?"

In the first half of the 19th century religious divisions in Lower Canada were uncomplicated: if you spoke French, you were Roman Catholic, if you

*Patrick Phelan, the first Irish pastor of the Recollect Church, was born in Ballyragget, County Killkenny in 1795 and joined the priesthood in Montreal in 1825. In the autumn of 1842 he was transferred to Bytown, now Ottawa, and shortly afterwards was made bishop of Kingston, Ont. He died there in 1862. When he left Montreal it was noted: "He was a man of remarkable personality, looked upon by all classes of the city with profound respect, and his departure was regretted by all his fellow citizens irrespective of race or creed."

spoke English you were Protestant. The soldiers who arrived with the British army were, for the most part, Protestants. Presbyterians built the first English-language church in Montreal in 1792. Anglicans worshipped at the old Jesuit chapel until 1814 when their first cathedral, Christ Church, was built just east of Place d'Armes on the north side of Notre Dame.

The single most important reason the Roman Catholic diocese would not build a church in Montreal for its English-speaking parishioners, however, had to do with money. The Irish didn't have any. They couldn't raise enough to support their own fabrique in Montreal. Under Quebec's *loi des fabriques,* the fabrique is the ecclesiastical corporation that represents the financial interests of a parish. The Irish often complained, "The French will not allow us to build a church ourselves, nor will they build one for us." The regulations governing fabriques were challenged in Quebec City in the early 1820s when Irish Catholics there began agitating for their own church. They were led by a rabble-rouser, Edmund Bailey O'Callahan, who managed to circumvent the bureaucracy. The cornerstone for Saint Patrick's in Quebec City's lower town was laid in 1832 and the first mass celebrated the following year. Three years later Pope Gregory XVI signed a bull making Montreal an autonomous diocese, and immediately hope of "building a church dedicated to Saint Patrick," was expressed in Montreal. The choice of patron saint was obvious: thought to be the son of a fifth-century Roman official posted to Wales, young Patricius was kidnapped by an Irish chieftain called Milchu, spent his adolescence in bondage as a shepherd slave, escaped, then went back to Ireland a priest to convert his captors. He is revered to this day for bringing hope to a people who dwell in despair.

A feasibility study was done for a church in his honour at the corner of St. Antoine and Hermine Streets across from the site of today's World Trade Centre. With the outbreak of the Rebellion of 1837 the project was suspended. Led by a political elite, disgruntled Canadian *patriotes* sought a republican form of government free from the oppression of the British Crown and took arms against the colonial authorities. During the conflict the Sulpicians considered the odds and recognised it was in their best political interest to remain loyal to the British. They helped to publish *L'Ami du Peuple,* a newspaper designed to defend British rule. Quiblier also used his personal influence with the Irish—who obviously had no great love for the British monarchy—to keep them from mobilizing in support of the *patriotes.* In fact because of Quiblier many enlisted with the British militia as volunteers.

The rebellion, poorly planned and badly led, was easily crushed. As a reward for their loyalty the Crown awarded the Sulpicians a generous land claims settlement. Under the deal they could draw from their Montreal properties an annuity income of 14 thousand British pounds each year.

Bishop Lartigue died in 1840 and was succeeded by his far more capable protégé, Ignace Bourget. Bourget was young, determined, and not afraid to use his position for political ends. He represented a real threat to the Sulpician hegemony on the island of Montreal. Originally from the Beauce, he was a product of the Pétit Séminaire du Québec, and was ordained in 1821, when he was only 22.He was also an ultramontasist—an ultra-conservative who believed in the supremacy of the church over the civil state, a church free from liberalising influences—who demanded absolute obedience to his own authority. The mantra he expected his people to follow was, "You listen to the curé, the curé listens to the bishop, the bishop listens to the Pope, the Pope listens to our Lord Jesus Christ, who aids with the Holy Spirit to render them infallible on the teaching and government of his Church." The Sulpicians marched to a different drummer. They were sympathetic to the Gallican doctrine that had taken root in France which held that papal authority was restricted by local canon and customs and civil law. Accordingly, they decided to consolidate their position on the Island of Montreal. With their annuity from the Crown the order's first priority was to build a church for the Irish almost as big as Notre Dame. It would be a supersymbolic gesture to establish the Sulpicians as the overwhelming presence in Montreal's Catholic community.

Saint Patrick's was conceived on the last Sunday of January 1841 when a dozen of the city's prominent Irish Catholics[*] met in the living room of one John Cassidy on Notre Dame St. to hear mass. Afterwards they began "devising methods for the erection of a new church sufficiently extensive for the accommodation of their Catholic brethren," and elected a building committee which drafted a petition with a stirring preamble and sent it to Quiblier. "We, the Roman Catholic inhabitants of the City of Montreal speaking the English language have long suffered from great inconveniences

---

[*]Patrick and James Brennan, Robert. J. Begly, Thomas Hewitt, John Cassidy, Thomas Battle, Peter Devine, Andrew Conlan, Thomas Neagle, Thomas McGrath, and John Monahan.

from want of accommodation in the churches appropriated for their use," they complained, "it having been noticed on several occasions that the poorer classes attended to their religious duties, even in the most rigorous season, outside the doors of the churches."

One week later, on February 8, Quiblier met the petitioners at O'Neill and Orr's Hotel on Place d'Armes and agreed to assume full responsibility for their project. Since the self-styled church wardens could not establish a fabrique and had no legal right to build a church by themselves they had little choice but to let him take over. As the minute books indicate, the committee resigned itself to the situation: "The greatest advantage will accrue from a co-operation with the (Sulpician) seminary in the proposed undertaking, and an equally thorough conviction that unity of purpose and co-operation with that institution will be the only means by which a church can be founded."

A budget of ten thousand pounds, worth about one million dollars in today's purchasing power, was agreed upon, and Quiblier wanted the congregation to raise one-third of the money before he would even consider building the church. "A stratagem was contrived by which, in subscribing our money to build the Saint Patrick's Church, we were led to believe we were building for ourselves," John Kelly, one of those present at the meeting, recalled later. In fact, even though the Irish were being asked to raise money for the church, the title to it would remain in the hands of the Sulpicians. Even more objectionable, the wardens of the parish church of Notre Dame—all of them French-speaking*—would at the same time be the wardens of Saint Patrick's chapel. From the outset, the wardens were not easily convinced that a separate church for the English was necessary when considerable work remained to be done on their own parish church. Quiblier worked out a compromise, and Bourget, who as bishop had to put his stamp of approval on the project, reluctantly agreed to the construction of a modest building. It would be a branch chapel or *succursale* of Notre Dame, and the civil register of all baptisms, marriages and funerals in the chapel would be kept at Notre Dame. The chapel was to be 180 by 90 feet, with no steeple, and no crypt. The conditions gave rise to a ditty:

---

*Alexis Laframboise, Q. Berthelet, A.N. Delisle, Louis Compte, John Donegan, Jean Bruneau, N.B. Doucet, E.M. Leprohon, Charles Rodier, L.B. Leprohon, Hubert Paré, and Albert Turin.

St. Patrick's is a funny place,
With lots of crazy people,
The curé wants to built a church,
But cannot have a steeple.

It is clear that from the outset Quiblier had a much more ambitious scheme in mind than either the building committee, the parish wardens, or the bishop. The initial plans for Saint Patrick's were probably derived from a sketch by a young British architect of French descent, Augustus Welby Northmore Pugin. Pugin set the pattern for Neo-Gothic revival with his designs for St. Chad's Cathedral in Birmingham and St. George's Cathedral in Southwark and had earned an international reputation with his book, *The True Principles of Painted or Christian Architecture*, published in 1841. It is telling that rather than engage a local architect for what was, after all, supposed to be a mere chapel, Quiblier sought the advice of one of the world's leading authorities.

"We are at the point of beginning to build a church in the Gothic style. It is hoped that it can accommodate eight to ten thousand people, about half of them in pews," Quiblier wrote to Pugin. "The severity of the climate and the heavy accumulation of snow during our long winters doesn't permit much exterior decoration, except perhaps for a few projecting panels. Do you have a plan for such a church that you would be able to send us without delay?" It seems he did. He was working on the English Jesuits' Church of the Immaculate Conception on Farm Street in South Kensington, London, and although there is no record of it, it is reasonable to suggest he gave Quiblier the courtesy of a reply.

On March 1, 1841, the building fund campaign was launched, and the Sulpicians tapped their impressive connections. The Bank of Montreal was the first to contribute—125 pounds. Prominent Anglicans John Molson and Peter McGill (whose wife was a Roman Catholic), both gave 25 pounds. The Governor General of British North America, Charles Edward Poulett-Thomson, 1st Baron Sydenham gave 20 pounds. He died in September and his successor, Charles Bagot, kicked in another 20 pounds. A third Governor General, Charles Theophilus, 1st Baron Metcalfe, was also tapped for ten pounds. Among the contributors were prominent members of Montreal's Jewish community. But raising money was hard. After two years of fund -

raising only 800 pounds had been collected. Only three families of the estimated 5,000 Irish Catholics in Montreal could afford to give more than ten pounds. Many parishioners were wary of contributing to a building that legally was not theirs. By July the building committee bought land for the church at the corner of St. Alexandre and de la Gauchetière, and met with Quiblier expecting construction to begin in September. According to the minutes of that meeting, Quiblier said, "There must be a misunderstanding as to the time for commencing the church, as it had been agreed between him and the deputation that the building should be commenced immediately this committee had raised the sum of 3,000 pounds and that until such a sum was raised he did not consider himself justified in taking a contract for this great work."

Montreal became the capital of the United Canadian Provinces in 1843 and this may have strengthened Quiblier's resolve to build a church befitting a capital city. He moved quickly to rescind the purchase of the site favoured by the building committee, and on May 18, 1843, he put a down payment on a choice piece of real estate—hill-top property that had been owned by fur trader Pierre Rastel Sieur de Rocheblave. Pascal Compte, a timber merchant, was hired as an architect and his brother Louis engaged as the building contractor. Quiblier was not above nepotism; Louis Compte was a warden of Notre Dame church. Alarmed because they were being bypassed at every turn, the Saint Patrick's building committee passed a resolution asking that Irish workmen be employed "in the execution of this great work as foremen, mechanics or labourers, that part of the population for whose use the church is intended." They also recommended that the building be contracted to the lowest tender. By June 12, 1843 Quiblier assured the building committee

> that every exertion would be used to complete the church as early as possible, that the greater part of the timber had been purchased and was seasoned and ready for immediate use, and that with the blessing of God he hoped the edifice would be sufficiently advanced for Divine service in the month of July 1845, on the first day of which he promised to offer up the sacrifice of the mass.

Three days later, on the feast of Corpus Christi, the building committee's minutes record that "a cross was placed on the spot at the head of the church intended as the site of the altar. The committee then pointed out to the people the extent of the intended church marked by pickets when the Reverend Gentleman said that nothing remains but to BUILD THIS CHURCH."

The Sulpicians honoured George III's consort by naming the bell in their parish church after her. When Saint Patrick's belfry was completed in 1846, the Sulpicians donated *La Vieille Charlotte* to the new church.
Courtesy of Saint Patrick's Basilica.

Chapter Two

IF SAINT PATRICK'S is owed to any one man it is to Josephe Vincent Quiblier. Without his vision and his reckless determination there would have been no church. He had to contend with opposition from all quarters, and as a result Saint Patrick's took four years to build instead of two. He argued with the bishop; his own wardens at Notre Dame balked at financing so costly a chapel when the towers of their own church were still under construction and its interior without decoration. The Irish building committee which had been largely excluded from the decision-making process became frustrated. Quiblier pressed on. When the building committee could not meet its fundraising objective, Quiblier hastily arranged a loan of 4,000 pounds on its behalf without informing its members. He also engaged new architects on his own, Félix Martin, a Jesuit priest, and Pierre-Louis Morin, a civil engineer and surveyor. Although Martin was an amateur architect, he was well versed in the English Gothic style and was familiar with the Jesuit church going up on Farm Street in London. His brother, Arthur, was an authority on the windows of Bourges Cathedral, and an expert on the restoration of Gothic cathedrals. Martin altered the approved design and made Saint Patrick's 50 percent bigger, which of course doubled the cost of the undertaking. Martin's plan was a model of simplicity—a great oblong hall, 233 by 105 feet, terminating in a horseshoe apse—a vast unadorned room, relatively cheap to finance and easy to build. It had no choir loft, no transepts or ambulatory. In keeping with the perpendicular 14th century French Gothic style, 12 pine pillars 25 meters tall swept the eye up the nave to the sanctuary. The plans also bear the mark of Quiblier's capricious improvisations. He added provisions for the spire which had been expressly prohibited by the bishop. The foundations for the belfry were to be contained behind the walls of the nave so that the diocesan office would not be aware that it was being built until construction was finished. Once the tower was up, a spire would have to be installed on top of it.

"Church wardens were not consulted in any way regarding the plan, size, or cost of site, and all the preliminaries were concealed from the Irish Catholics who were denied the opportunity of an opinion respecting them," John Kelly complained. Once the plans for the church were drawn, interminable wrangling followed over who would be contracted to build it. The Compte brothers had recruited French Canadian construction crews for the project against the committee's specific instructions that Irish labourers be used. When the Comptes ignored the building committee's suggestion, the self-styled wardens demanded the contractors be fired, and that "in consequence of the difficulty experienced by the Messrs in selecting labourers according to the recommendation of the committee, it was resolved that Messrs Thomas McNaughton and Charles Curran should be appointed to issue orders to the applicants for employment."

To satisfy the building committee Quiblier drew up a revised list of contractors and the Comptes were demoted to the role of sub-contractors. About 200 people, about two-thirds of them Irish, were hired for the project at the going wages: "Foremen five shillings per diem, labourers, two shillings six pence, and that for the use of a cart, horse and man, the sum of four shillings and six pence a day shall be allowed." On average, labourers made 60 cents a day, stone masons around $1 a day.

The seven cornerstones for Saint Patrick's were blessed on September 26, 1843, before a crowd of 10,000 on what the *Gazette* described as a day "of pleasure and rejoicing to the Irish inhabitants of Montreal and one of agreeable interest to the community of large." Bishop Ignace Bourget placed the first stone, and with words that would return to bedevil him, he dedicated the building "as an exclusive centre of worship for Catholics of the English language." The speaker of the Canadian Parliament and one of the first francophone businessmen to become successful in British commerce and colonial politics, Augustin Cuvillier tapped the second one with a hammer. Montreal's mayor, Joseph Bourret, laid the third, and Judge Rolland, representing the city's judiciary, the fourth stone. The fifth was placed by Benjamin Holmes and the remaining two by representatives of the Hibernian Benevolent Society and the Temperance Society.

Work on the church began immediately that autumn. Limestone was carted from the quarry at Mile End. Eight months later, by May 1844, the progress report indicated that the "foundation was now sunk to a sufficient depth, say on the northeast side, 17 feet, on the south west side, 21 feet, and that they will commence the masterwork in a day or two." The walls, four feet thick, began to rise by winch and crane and block and tackle. For the first two years work was suspended during the winter months until 1845 when the shell was enclosed. French-speaking foremen directed the operations, much to the annoyance of the Irish labourers. "We Irish Catholics were so completely excluded from any participation that great dissatisfaction was felt and expressed," Kelly wrote. "John Huston was appointed mason foreman on the work, but he was the only Irishman who had any position of authority in connection with the building except John Ward, he who had done the plaster work." Occasionally, accidents claimed lives. The *Gazette* reported the death of one labourer who "met with a blow from a stone which he was raising by which his scull was fractured. He was an Irishman, a respectable and sober man, and was commonly called Sim."

A storm in October of 1846 played havoc with the construction site. "Several casualties have occurred in and around Montreal, but so far as we have heard, in no case have been attended with loss of life," said the *Gazette*. "But a house was unroofed in the neighbourhood of Saint Patrick's church and several wooden buildings were blown down upon farms in the vicinity."

John Kelly frequently visited the building site and grew increasing anxious about the mounting cost of the project. "From close observation I made up my mind that the work must have cost nearly double as much as it was done by the day, as the same kind of work could have been done by contract. I concluded that the building of Saint Patrick's Church must have cost from 60 to 70 percent more than its real value." Kelly's evaluation was something of an exaggeration. The contractor's books show the church cost 24,060 pounds, or about $2.5 million in today's money, about 25 percent more than had been budgeted. The wardens grew ever more recalcitrant and the cost over-runs provoked a showdown between Bourget and Quiblier. The bishop had had enough of Quiblier's insubordination. Just as Quiblier's third term as head of his community was drawing to a close, Bourget demanded obedience from all of his priests. He successfully persuaded the Sulpicians that Quiblier had mismanaged their affairs and Quiblier's authority was so undermined within his religious community that he had no choice but to resign, which he did, on April 21, 1846. One of his biographers, Louis Rousseau, says that after he quit it had been his wish to stay at the seminary in Montreal for the rest of his life, "but the process which led him to resign created such a climate of opinion within the house, and among the public, that he thought it wiser to leave in October for Europe." He was sent to England by his successor, Pierre-Louis Billaudèle, where he worked for the next five years.[*]

By September 1846, the prohibited belfry of Saint Patrick's was completed and in December the Sulpicians donated *La Vieille Charlotte*, the bell that had been in the old parish church on Place d'Armes, to Saint Patrick's. The 2,250-pound bell had been cast in Whitechapel in England in 1774. It was unusual in that it had silver in its composition. A 200-pound bell, *Sanctus*, was also installed. Once the bells were positioned, plans to add the mid-wall shaft between the belfry and the spire were abandoned. It is 40 feet shorter than it should be, and as a result the steeple has a rather stumpy appearance.

The Reverend Father Joseph Connolly was appointed church administrator, which in effect made the 31-year-old Sulpician the first pastor of Saint Patrick's. Connolly was born in Carrick-on-Suir, Ireland, March 8, 1816 and joined the Sulpician order in France. He came to Canada in 1843 and was ordained in Montreal the following year. He was made pastor not because he was Irish, and not because he possessed outstanding administrative abilities, nor because he was ambitious, but because he was one of the few priests in Montreal who was fluent in English.

Saint Patrick's was blessed on the feast of its namesake, March 17, 1847. The inauguration attracted huge crowds. According to one account in the Sulpician archives,

> the parade was grand and impressive for the opening service, the church was wholly inadequate for the crowd seeking entrance. It was estimated that 4,000 were within its walls and as many more without.
>
> Mass was celebrated solemnly with music, (God Save the Queen) by Bishop Jean-Charles Prince, the comptroller of the diocese, and Mr. Connolly gave a pathetic sermon

[*]Quiblier died in Issy les Moulineaux, France on September 12, 1852.

The Reverend Joseph Connolly was appointed church administrator in 1846, which in effect made the 31-year-old Sulpician the first pastor of Saint Patrick's.
Photo by William Notman. Courtesy of Saint Patrick's Basilica.

Saint Patrick's Church, 1853.
"Placed almost on Montreal's highest point (excepting the mountain),
it dominates the city."
Notman Photographic Archives of the McCord Museum of Canadian History.

which went on for over an hour. The day, however, is certainly a memorable one for the Irish of the city, the sheer size of the building evidence of their faith and their determination. Only the parish church is more beautiful. The interior is noble and elegant, even if it is not finished.

In the minute book for the parish of Notre Dame, Bishop Prince scrawled a concise entry:

> We went in procession at 8 a.m. from the parochial church to the new church, splendidly built in the St. Lawrence suburb, and there in the presence of an extraordinary large number of the faithful we solemnly blessed the new building under the patronage of St. Patrick, confessor, Pontiff and Apostle of Ireland.

A reporter with the *Journal de Québec* thought the church was

> heavy and lacks elegance. However, one must not conclude that Saint Patrick's is not a handsome building. Placed almost on Montreal's highest point, (excepting the mountain) it dominates all the city. It is considerably smaller than the parish church. If the exterior of the latter is more majestic, the new temple has a finer interior through the bravery and simple elegance of its form, by the life and odour of religious fervor which seizes you when you walk under its beautifully naked vault.

Not everyone was impressed. Napoléon Bourassa, a leading Quebec architect, critic, and interior decorator who specialised in religious art, thought the church too big for its location.

> When I look at this great stone thing perched so naively on a hill and exposed to the mercy of the four winds, it seems to me it wasn't built where it stands, but that workmen assembled it elsewhere like a caterer who is asked to throw a pie together. It seems to me that they didn't realise until

they installed it that it would be so exposed and so heavy for its base.

It looks as if they had to hack away bits of it to get it up the hill, slicing off anything that would interfere with transporting it, and that gives it such a pitiful air. It looks like they only left the front intact and stuck on the back part. Then there's that procession across the front of four or six obelisks that look like curved cement pickles or petrified pom-poms on a hat waiting for a big enough chef to put it on his head. You could get rid of them and not lose a thing.

The church dominates a painting of the Montreal skyline done by John Murray shortly after it opened, and which now hangs in the Château de Ramezay. The tin roof gleams in the afternoon sunlight. The church is at the centre of a pastoral scene, towering above the surrounding orchards, meadows, and green fields.

Saint Patrick's was in a haphazard, make-shift state, still in the process of becoming. It was one cavernous hall with impromptu piecemeal decor. The walls were hung with 14 oversized paintings of the Way of the Cross by Quebec artist Antoine Plamondon. The paintings had been commissioned by the Sulpicians for Notre Dame seven years earlier, but Quiblier rejected them as being "historically inaccurate." Having paid for them, however, he relegated them to a little-used corridor in the seminary before fobbing them off on Saint Patrick's. The correspondent who covered the opening of the church for the *Journal de Québec* was, however, "agreeably surprised to discover the fourteen paintings of the Passion by our artist, Mr. Plamondon," in the church.

> I found myself again in front of these beautiful paintings which have lost none of their freshness and the magnificence of colouring that made them so much admired. Why then have they been left so long in a neglected corridor, prey to humidity and deterioration when horrible scabs of paintings cover the walls of almost all the churches in this district, insulting rather than adorning the majesty of their surroundings?

There wasn't much stained glass to look at. There were four windows in the apse behind the altar; but they were of ordinary coloured glass that came from France and may have been a gift from Quiblier. But in spite of the rudimentary decoration most visitors were impressed by the interior.

According to one parishioner who wrote on the day after the church was blessed:

> Although a great deal yet remains to be done to complete the fitting up of the building, the interior architecture is chaste and elegant in its style, very lofty, and well lighted by a vast quantity of long narrow windows, beautifully decorated and stained, yet so as not to obscure rays of light.
>
> The absence of all interior garniture, with the exception of that which is absolutely necessary, gives the interior the fabric of an airy and roomy appearance. No pews are yet constructed and for some time to come, at any rate, we are informed there will be none.

Chapter Three

No sooner had Saint Patrick's opened its doors than death came calling. On Monday, June 7, 1847, three merchant ships, the *Queen*, the *Rowland Hill*, and *Québec*, their holds crammed with 2,304 refugees fleeing the Great Famine in Ireland, tied up in the Montreal waterfront. Irish tenant farmers had become totally dependent on the potato for their livelihoods; when a virulent fungus destroyed their crops in 1846, the disaster was immediate. Farmers who couldn't pay rent to their British landlords were evicted. They had three choices: starvation, emigration, or a solution called "taking the soup," which required Roman Catholics to convert if they hoped to qualify for aid from Protestant relief agencies. An estimated two million, or one quarter of the island's population, were forced to leave. More died of disease aboard the "coffin ships" that brought them to America than died of starvation.

One week after the vessels arrived an ominous story appeared in the *Gazette*:

> Emigrant sheds are reported as much overcrowded and deaths numerous. A wharf on Windmill Point for the separate use of immigrants is recommended. From what we can gather ... the prevailing disease seems to be low typhoid fever, and the fatal cases are mostly those on whom the peculiar local influences either of air or water, cause, when in a state of debility, dysentery.

The first of the priests from Saint Patrick's to die was Father Patrick Morgan on July 8. He was only 32. Two days later, Father Lawrence McInerney died, then Father Remi Carof on July 12, and on July 15 Father Pierre Richard, who was only 30 and who had been recently ordained. Father John Jackson Richards, a convert from Virginia, died on July 23, almost 34 years to the day he was ordained a priest. He was 68. The only other priest attached to Saint Patrick's, Father James McMahon was assigned to New York, and later to Washington, D.C. where he helped to found Catholic University. That, observed the *Gazette,* left Father Connolly as "the only clergyman left speaking the English language who is able to visit the sheds. Four hundred emigrant children are now being taken care of by Les Dames du Bon Pasteur, and other religious institutions of this city. All the hospitals attached to the religious institutions are full." Each Monday the Montreal newspapers published the weekly returns of internments. The report dated June 22, 1847: Boys 29, Married Men, 10, Bachelors, 7; Girls, 22, Married women 4, Unmarried Women, 4.

Connolly's world was saturated with death. The typhus gave a dark resonance to his days. The meticulous entries in the day books he had kept for years in his crabbed handwriting listing births deaths and marriages, abruptly stops that summer. On Sunday, July 25, 1847, he mounted the pulpit and, extending his hands, lamented, "Here I am, here I stand, the bird alone."

Connolly resisted all attempts to portray him as a hero and often recalled that he simply did his job. "If I prepared for death and consigned to the silent grave for a period of six weeks or more 50 adult persons a day, I was but doing what every priest would be bound to do under similar circumstances," he said. "I was discharging my sacred duty; and if of all the clergymen who commenced at the beginning and laboured to the end of that dire visitation I was the only survivor, it makes me tremble, lest I alone should be found unworthy of the reward to which they were called in the midst of their labours."

In all, six priests—the five curates from Saint Patrick's, the vicar of the diocese, Hyacinthe Hudon—and seven Grey Nuns died that summer.[*] Montreal's Mayor John Easton Mills was another victim. Bishop Bourget was stricken, too, but recovered. Even the *Gazette,* usually indifferent to Catholics in its pages, was moved to admire the selfless devotion.

> The exertions of the Roman Catholic clergy are unwearied
> by fatigue and undeterred by danger. The Right Reverend

[*]Sister Adeline Limoges, Sister Angélique Chevrefils-Primeau, Sister Jeannette Collins, Sister Marie-Rose Barbeau, Sister Adolie Bruyère, Sister Charlotte Ste. Croix Pomainville and Sister Anne Nobles.

the Bishop of the Diocese and his Vicar General spend
alternate nights in watching in the pestilential atmosphere
over the sick and the dying. There never, surely, was any
church which in times of most fiery persecution, proved
at the sacrifice of comfort and life, its devotion to religious
duty, and to what it believes to be religious truth, more
signally than does now the Roman Catholic Clergy of
Montreal.

It is estimated 75,000 people fleeing the famine in Ireland came to
Canada and of them, 30,000 died including at least 6,000 at sea, as many as
8,000 at Grosse Ile, perhaps 6,000 in Quebec City, and another 6,000
thousand in Montreal. Those who died in the sheds at Pointe St. Charles
are buried anonymously in a mass grave which is today marked by a
lugubrious black stone in the middle of Bridge St. leading to the
embankment of Victoria Bridge. A visiting Irish priest who saw the rock in
1870 wrote of the burial ground: "There was the desolate spot, enclosed
by a fragile paling—there the numerous mounds—and above all, in the
centre, an enormous stone placed on a pedestal—a huge boulder from the
bed of the St. Lawrence—commemorating the tragic circumstances, with
words somewhat as follows: 'Here lie the remains of 6,000 immigrants.
(*Why did they not say Irish?*) who perished in 1847.'" It took 150 years for a
memorial tablet to those who died during Black '47 to be installed in Saint
Patrick's. Before it was dedicated on February 16, 1997, the only Roman
Catholic church in the city to commemorate the immigrant dead was Notre
Dame de Bonsecours. After his recovery from the disease, Bishop Bourget
declared the mariner's chapel a centre of devotion for those who survived
the plague. There, inside the main entrance on the ceiling under the choir
loft is a mural that depicts four Grey Nuns and a priest believed to be
Father Richards attending to the dead and dying. But if you didn't know it
was there, you'd miss it. You have to look up and crane your neck to see it.

In truth, perhaps one of the reasons it took so long for a memorial to
go up in Saint Patrick's is because the Irish already in Montreal who built
the church didn't especially welcome the immigrants who survived the
Great Hunger. Class distinctions within the Irish community were
pronounced. Those who came in the 1820s and had prospered in Canada

distanced themselves from the Famine Irish and their destitute roots. Nevertheless, because they were Roman Catholics, almost all of the Irish in the city were automatically excluded from the Protestant, English-speaking ruling class. The Irish immigrant stock was confined to what became known as the City Below the Hill. It was these people who first made Saint Patrick's a source of solace, hope, and exaltation, the organic heart of their community, until 1850 when St. Ann's was built for them in Griffintown.

The typhus epidemic left Saint Patrick's with only one priest. Bishop Bourget invited the Jesuits back to Montreal, then the Oblates of Mary Immaculate, to provide reinforcements and to recruit allies to help him break the Sulpician monopoly on the island. The Jesuits were seconded to Saint Patrick's until 1864 when they built their own church nearby, the Gésu on de Bleury. The Sulpicians, meanwhile were not idle. They set up a department of English-Speaking Affairs, and dispatched their former superior, Josephe Quiblier from London to Ireland to find a suitable candidate to take charge of the office. Quiblier found his recruit in Drogheda, in the archdiocese of Armagh. Father Patrick Dowd ultimately would be Quiblier's most important legacy to the church he had built.

A good and decent man of superior intelligence and unlimited energy, Dowd was born in Dunleer, County Louth on November 24, 1812. He studied at the Irish College of Paris, was ordained in France in May 1837, and returned to begin his ministry in Ireland. "I was happy at home, not even the slightest shadow of pain crossed my path. God was always too good to me," Dowd once said "He favoured me with the full hearted bliss of a child in the house of its father during the whole of my career at home, as a boy, a student, and as a young priest." The story goes that when Quiblier approached the primate of Ireland for permission to hire the 35-year-old priest, the archbishop agreed reluctantly, saying, "You are asking for my own heart." Father Dowd arrived to begin work in the United Canadian Provinces in June 28, 1848. He was not totally unfamiliar with Montreal; one of his cousins, Father Patrick Morgan was a victim of the typhus epidemic. Dowd's first years on the job were trying. He focused on the social problems. At least one thousand children had been orphaned by the epidemic and many young women were left widowed and destitute. To escape the desolation in their lives they turned to drink and to prostitution.

Montreal, which had 600 taverns in 1846, had 1,200 three years later—one tavern for every seven men in the city! Alcoholism was rampant. Dowd recognised that women were the heart of the church and helped organise the Ladies of Charity who held their first strawberry social and parish bazaar in October 1849. Over the next 35 years the bazaars raised an astonishing $136,000 for charity. He set up St. Patrick's Orphan Asylum in 1851, and turned what was to have been the priests' rectory, the old de Rochblave mansion, next to Saint Patrick's Church into a refuge for women, St. Bridgit's.* He worked with the city to open St. Patrick's hospital in 1852. He was also responsible for having the auxiliary chapel of St Ann's, built on Basin Street for the Irish in Griffintown. There would have been a third chapel, St. Bridgit's, for the Irish who had gravitated to Montreal's east-end Hochelaga district, but the plans for that chapel were vetoed by Bishop Bourget, who was becoming concerned that the number of immigrants was beginning to pose a threat to "The French Canadian race."

The political atmosphere in Montreal at the time was volatile; tension between French and English in the capital ran high. In 1849 an angry mob set fire to the parliament buildings in St. Ann's Market (today Place d'Youville). As a consequence the capital was split between Quebec City and Toronto. In 1851 Montreal was hit with bubonic plague. After that, fire destroyed most of Griffintown. The city seemed doomed. As one Boston newspaper put it, "Montreal wears a dismal aspect. The population has decreased some thousands, and the removal of the government caused some four thousand more to leave ... The fate of Sodom and Gomorrah appears to hang over the city."

Dowd's energy and appetite for work seemed inexhaustible. He proved himself deeply compassionate, warm and self-deprecating. He spoke immpeccable Parisian French with an Irish brogue and was a consummate orator. Soon, to the envy of of his episcopal colleagues, he figured prominently in the plans of his Sulpician superiors. He was so capable an administrator and perhaps so potential a threat to the diocese that Bishop Bourget recommended that Dowd be appointed coadjutor bishop of Toronto. Pius IX issued the necessary bulls on December 17, 1852, but

---

*In 1869 it was replaced by St. Bridgit's Asylum and Night Refuge at the corner of de la Gauchetière and Beaver Hall Hill. The refuge became the Father Dowd Memorial Home in 1928. The building was condemned and torn down in 1977.

On June 28, 1848 Father Dowd arrived from Ireland to begin work in the
United Canadian Provinces. He became Saint Patrick's second pastor in 1859.
He proved himself deeply compassionate, warm, and self-deprecating.
Photo by William Notman. Courtesy of Saint Patrick's Basilica.

Dowd refused to be served with them. Under canon law at the time, papal bulls had to be delivered in person and placed in the hands of the priest to whom they were addressed. Dowd went to Paris for a six-month vacation to avoid acknowledging receiving the letter. When the Vatican attempted to forward the documents to him in Paris, he came back to Montreal. It took some doing, but eventually he convinced Rome he was not interested in a promotion; his duty was to his parish in Montreal. Later he was offered the bishop's seat in Kingston and Halifax but also turned down those positions.

In 1853, Saint Patrick's was at the eye of a storm for which no one was prepared. That summer a defrocked Italian priest named Alessandro Gavazzi went on a tour of North America and stirred emotions with his rolling tirades against Catholicism. Catholics saw him as a heretic and traitor; Protestants took to him as a spellbinding evangelist. When he came to speak in Lower Canada, Gavazzi was booed from the pulpit in Quebec City on June 6, 1853. He was warned that his presence in Montreal could only lead to hostility, but three days later he arrived for a rally at Zion Church, a block and a half from Saint Patrick's. Father Connolly had urged his parishioners to ignore Gavazzi, and to let him have his say. However, a mob of Roman Catholic vigilantes from Griffintown roared up Beaver Hall Hill, determined to break up Gavazzi's service. As they tried to storm Zion Church Gavazzi inflamed the situation. "I am under the British lion, and not under papal keys," he thundered to his audience. "If you allow such rabble to get their own way of it, then you will not be governed by the Canadian constitution but by Jesuits and priests."

With that, shots were fired and a riot broke out. Eleven people were killed. The *Gazette* blamed those who worshipped at Saint Patrick's. "These were all Irishmen, for the French Canadians, to their honour be it said, have never shown any wish to interfere in matters of religion, but on the contrary have yielded to all the same privileges they enjoy themselves," read the paper's account.

> Resistance was made against the ruffians, and the police stepped forward to prevent their effecting an entrance, but they were overpowered by the Roman Catholics. Some of the people now inside the church rushed out, and driving

the Roman Catholics back followed them a short distance. Satisfied with repulsing their assailants they returned to the church, but the Roman Catholics seeing them retire, renewed their assault. One of the Roman Catholics fired a pistol when he was immediately shot by a Protestant who observed him, but not dead.

Gavazzi barely managed to escape with his life. He fled to Laprairie, never to return to Montreal.

The Gavazzi furore was soon forgotten, but a new and much more dangerous menace appeared on the horizon to disrupt the social order— the Fenians. The Fenians grew out of a secret society, the Hearts of Steel, formed in Ireland to protect priests from the penal laws. Over time, more militant branches sworn to uphold Irish ethnicity and wreak revenge on the British evolved. In America these groups surfaced under different names, the Molly Maguires, the Ancient Order of Hibernians, and the Fenians. The Fenians were underground terrorists based in New England, intent on invading the Canadian provinces to liberate them from British oppression. They were making headway among the Irish in Canada. The Sulpicians wanted a dynamic leader to tackle the threat head-on. By then Father Dowd had become the *de facto* spiritual leader of the Irish in Montreal. He had proven that he was as concerned about his congregation's health and physical well-being as he was about its spiritual welfare. He had built a reputation as a priest who may have been feisty and strict, but who was always fair. He had strength and independence of mind, an engaging, frank manner, and a devotion to helping the dispossessed. His profile in the community was high. The time had come to reward him with Saint Patrick's. There was, however one obstacle—the church already had a pastor, Joseph Connolly, and he was not anxious to be shunted out. When the Sulpicians reassigned Connolly without reason or explanation, he balked. Connolly was indignant not only because he thought that he had earned his sinecure at Saint Patrick's during the typhus epidemic but because he was too experienced to be pushed aside. According to historian John Loye, the excuse used to remove Connolly was an incident that occurred during a visit to Saint Patrick's by a Bishop from France. At one point in the service the bishop came to the communion rail to speak to the congregation while Father Connolly was conducting the choir. "The Bishop raised his hand for silence, and although his attention had been drawn to it," Loye suggests Father Connolly "ignored the Bishop's repeated sign and continued to the conclusion of the hymn. This action, it was said, sealed his fate."

The day Connolly left Saint Patrick's he also quit the Sulpicians, citing "a deep sense of duty" to do so. "However painful to the congregation may be the separation, it is not less painful to me, and you judge correctly in supposing that nothing but a sense of obedience could prevail on me to take a step productive of such pain to the congregation and myself," he wrote to his superior. Father Connolly left Montreal for self-imposed exile in Boston. Friends who visited him there later described him as profoundly unhappy. "When you leave Montreal," he told them, "you will never find another Montreal."

He died in Boston on September 16, 1863.

Chapter Four

FATHER DOWD BECAME the second pastor of Saint Patrick's in December 1859. "He had two peculiarities," an old friend recalled. "No matter how intemperate the weather, or how cold it might be, he never wore anything but cotton socks and he never used gloves. No matter where you might meet him, you would never find him gloved." His qualities of leadership were put to the test almost as soon as he took over as pastor. The United States was on the brink of civil war, and in November 1861 an American warship intercepted the British steamship *Trent* in international waters and removed two Confederate spies. Britain denounced the violation and the Canadian provinces were no less outraged. Tempers flared. Montreal seethed with unrest and anxiety. "If we are embroiled in a war not directly provoked by us … we are called upon by every interest, every feeling of honour and patriotism and affection for the Old Flag to do our very utmost for defence," editorialised the *Gazette*. The Canadian provinces were especially vulnerable to an attack from the United States and set out to raise a militia. Most of the city's Irish despised the British and the Old Flag. In fact, the United States was the first choice for the majority of the Irish emigrants. The only reason so many wound up in Canada was because fares to Quebec were subsidised and therefore cheaper than those to the United States. Then, at the height of the potato famine, Washington restricted Irish immigration and thousands more wound up by default in Canada. Dowd faced a ticklish situation. His challenge was to get his Irish charges to enlist in the British army without making it appear he was taking sides. He was fortunate to have in his congregation Thomas D'Arcy McGee, a prominent journalist who had left Ireland for the United States in 1842, proudly boasting that he was "a traitor to the British government." McGee had however, gradually become disillusioned south of the border and in the spring of 1857 moved to Montreal where he found much more freedom to express "private, social, religious and political opinion." He started a newspaper and was elected as a Liberal to represent Montreal in the National Assembly. By 1862 he had become a Conservative and began advocating the idea of an independent British-American nation. "We have no right to intrude our Irish patriotism on this soil, for our first duty is to the land where we live and where we must find the true sphere of our duties," McGee argued. "While always ready therefore to say the right word and do the right act for the land of my forefathers, I am bound above all to Canada, the land where I reside."

The pastoral letter read in the church on Sunday, January 5, 1862 urged the Irish to support the British in the *Trent* affair. The letter was almost certainly drafted by McGee and Dowd. "It is not now a question for the volunteers to shed their blood on the frontiers as war with our neighbours has not yet even been declared, and may not be especially if they perceive that Canada has many strong arms well disciplined for defence," it read. "We incur therefore, less risk of war by enrolling in large numbers and with heartiness than if we stood with our arms folded as cowards and loiterers generally do." Forced to choose between compliance to the colonial authorities or risk open hostility, the majority of Montreal's Irish went along with the church's position and enlisted in the Prince's Own Militia Regiment. They never saw action. President Abraham Lincoln, not eager to fight a war on two fronts, released the hostages, and the crisis was defused.

Together, the hard-drinking McGee and Father Dowd were an unbeatable combination. Both came from County Louth, and together they played both sides of the street with acuity. Dowd supported McGee's political ambitions, and McGee endorsed Dowd's religious initiatives. They were instrumental in splitting Montreal's non-sectarian St. Patrick's Society into two groups — the St. Patrick's Society for the Catholics, and The Irish Benevolent Society for the Protestants. The division came because not because of any religious animosity between the two groups, but because Dowd did not want the Protestants to be party to any of the infighting that went on within the Catholic community. He made certain, however, that the two organisations worked together in community projects, and each year Dowd personally remained in charge of the arrangements for the St. Patrick's Day Parade. He insisted it not be called a "parade" but a "procession." For many years it ended with the Prince's Own Militia Regiment Brass Band marching up the centre aisle of the church.

When Dowd became pastor of Saint Patrick's, it was an enormous building, cold and barren, with mismatched altars. In 1861 the Sulpicians engaged the master woodcarver Victor Bourgeau to design a pulpit*, build a choir loft, and remodel the altars. Bourgeau's great achievement would be the interior decoration of Notre Dame, but the prototype was Saint Patrick's. There was nothing extravagant about his embellishments. They reflected Dowd's modest taste. His priority was to have 300 pews installed "made of the best clear pine with neatly panelled ends and doors, with bookrests of black walnut." The pews were rented to parishioners. Those who wished to sit immediately below the pulpit paid $20 a year for the privilege; the cheapest pews at the rear of the church went for $5 a year. The altars were completely redone and the reredos installed. *La Minerve* described the work in its edition of March 18, 1862: "The choir loft is now entirely decorated with stained glass, colourful paint and gold leaf. The two side chapels dedicated to St. Joseph and the Virgin Mary are decorated in a manner similar to the choir loft. The cornices of the pilasters are very ornate and so are the pilasters themselves. Finally, aside from the altar which is a massive wooden structure 60 feet high and 20 feet across, sculptured, painted and decorated with gold, the choir loft too is embellished with stalls surmounted with a canopy and enriched with decorations befitting the rest of the church. The decorated wooden structure takes up 9,000 square feet. In the middle are two 14-foot side altars topped with wide arcades. There are also 82 small statues. The lovely stained glass in the sanctuary and the rose clerestory windows are the work of Montreal's Grey Nuns."

The eight clerestory windows still to be seen are, in fact, the work of Sister Adine Desjardins. What is remarkable is that Sister Desjardins had no formal training in art, painting, or stained glass work. She also supervised the creation of four windows that were installed in the apse behind the altar. They depicted scenes from the Bible, such as the Return of the Prodigal Son. The Grey Nuns' bill for the work came to $3,000.

Critic Napoléon Bourassa was still not impressed. While he admitted it was an improvement over what had been, he didn't think much of the reredos. Bourassa referred to the ornamental screens behind the altars as

*Bourgeau's pulpit in Saint Patrick's was originally suspended from the third pillar in the nave, almost in the centre of the church. It was moved to where it is now in 1893.

little more than "shelving units with French Gothic touches, painted in every colour under the sun, an astonishing hodge-podge of architectural elements, heavy and light, colliding with and pushing up against each other a dizzy array of frames, buttresses, fret work, gables, balustrades, pedestals, and niches—all that just to display 64 plaster men."

The statues behind the high altar were to have been arranged according to an iconographic design, the largest on the top being those of Celtic saints: Patrick of Ireland flanked by Columba of Iona, Bridgit of Kildare, Margaret of Scotland, and Martin of Tours. The tier below them was to have been reserved for the patron saint of Montreal, Mary, Canada's patron, St. Joseph, Quebec's patron, St. Anne, and the patron saint of French Canada, St. John the Baptist. Beneath them, at the tabernacle level, were to be saints with a local devotional following such as St. Gabriel, St. Roch, St. Monica and St. Ciarán of Saigher, the first Irish-born saint. But by the time the decor was complete, the design concept had been ignored; today most of the 86 statues on the three altars are generic. When the statues arrived, they proved to be too small for their niches so they were mounted on wooden blocks. St. Patrick presides over the arrangement, of course, but the precise order of the other saints was never executed and today no one is quite certain which are which. Some, such as Thérèse of Lisieux, Anthony of Padua, Francis Xavier, St. Roch, and Marguerite Bourgeoys, are easily identified by their accessories, and others by the instruments of their martyrdom. It is impossible, however, to put names to all of them.

Bourgeau's work was only the beginning; it was obvious further decoration had to be done. According to church records, "Father Dowd thought the rest of the work could be completed for about $4,000 and suggested that this amount could be raised by means of a lottery for which purpose he offered his watch (a valuable gold one) the tickets to be 2'6 (50 cents) each so as to place them within the reach of every member of the congregation. The raffle was held on March 17, 1865, and the winning number was held by Edward Burns of St. Maurice Street.

The proceeds from the draw were used to complete the job. A French priest who had studied interior decoration, Etienne Michel Faillon, painted the walls in shades of beige and the ceiling deep blue, with gold stars. The paintings of the Annunciation and the Death of St. Joseph above the lateral side altars were acquired. They are copies of works by 17th-century French painter Eustache Le Sueur. The Annunciation cost $250, the death of St. Joseph, $300.

Once they had the church the way they wanted it and were beginning to feel secure in their place of worship, the parishioners received a rude awakening. They were shocked to learn that Bishop Bourget had designs of his own on Saint Patrick's: he planned to expropriate the chapel from the Sulpicians and to take it away from the Irish.

Chapter Five

TWENTY YEARS AFTER Ignace Bourget dedicated Saint Patrick's as "an exclusive centre of worship for the English language," he attempted to assimilate its congregation by making Saint Patrick's a French-language parish and dispersing its Irish anglophone congregation. On Sunday, November 25, 1866, Father Dowd mounted the pulpit and read a pastoral letter outlining the bishop's plans to create three new "integrated" parishes in the diocese. Bourget's idea was to carve the new parishes out of Notre Dame parish. The scheme would, in effect, disperse most of the 30,000 anglophones who worshipped at Saint Patrick's among six French-speaking churches. Bourget's aim in establishing new boundaries was to reduce the English to a minority in all three of the proposed new parishes. To be fair to the bishop, some kind of reorganisation was long overdue. Notre Dame parish covered 55 square miles. Smaller parishes would be easier to manage than the system of branch chapels that had been devised by the Sulpicians. One of the difficulties with the branch chapels was that all births, marriages, and deaths were kept in a central registry at Notre Dame and as the city grew, keeping the registry had become cumbersome. Bourget had announced his intention to eliminate branch chapels in 1864 and the Sacred Congregation for the Propagation of the Faith in Rome agreed a better system was required. Pope Pius IX issued the appropriate apostolic decree authorising the bishop to proceed. Under his plan, Saint Patrick's parish would shrink to the size of a postage stamp between Sherbrooke and St. Antoine Streets, bounded by Mountain on the west and de Bleury to the east.

Father Dowd was not, however, about to surrender Saint Patrick's without a fight. Six special circumstances, he argued, rendered Bourget's plan unacceptable.

First, the church was built by the Sulpicians, not the diocese;

Second, the Sulpicians enlisted and received help from the English-speaking parishioners to finance and build it;

Third, the Sulpicians "furnished for its construction $40,000, and have not indicated their intention of changing the destiny of the church;"

Fourth, the congregation itself spent $30,000 to decorate the church;

Fifth, the church was blessed and dedicated by Bishop Bourget himself as a chapel for the English, and

Sixth, with the bishop's own consent, "that of the fabrique and that of the seminary and of all those who are concerned," English-speaking Catholics "had enjoyed peaceful possession of Saint Patrick's church without interruption from the day of its opening until the present day—a period of 20 years."

Bourget wouldn't budge. The Irish, he pointed out, were a minority in the diocese and as such should be grateful for the favours the Church had done for them. "Count if you are able, all the works undertaken for the Irish people of which We have been the life and the promoter. When the ravages of typhus left the children of your unfortunate countrymen orphans on our shores, didn't We find parents to adopt them, raise them and cherish them as their own?" he reminded them in a letter. "Not only that," he wrote, "charity obliged us to do more for these children, the sight of whose suffering touched Our paternal heart. Did we not set up in their behalf seminaries, colleges, convents and charitable institutions?"

Not only Father Dowd, but Thomas D'Arcy McGee was incensed. It was, McGee countered in a letter of reply on December 2, not the diocese but the Sulpicians who deserved the credit for nurturing the Irish.

> In Montreal our Pastors have a glorious history of 200 years. Through that long period, in an unbroken succession of holy, learned and devoted priests, they have laboured for the glory of God and the salvation of souls. They watched over the infant church of Montreal, and they have fostered it into its present majestic proportions.
>
> Out of their immense wealth they reserve for themselves a pittance; the rest they lavish, but with prudent hand, on works of religion, of charity and of education. Two centuries of unremitting labour, of unblemished reputation, and of ever increasing zeal and devotedness appear to us a

sufficient test of the true spirit that alienates our beloved
Pastors.

McGee was blunt: "We do not wish to be ungrateful; neither do we
desire to acknowledge personal obligations which we do not owe. We
certainly are not aware that any one of the churches or charitable institutions
destined for the benefit of the Irish have originated with or received any
particular aid from your lordship." McGee then accused Bourget of insulting
the Irish. "Your Lordship, referring to the sad events of 1847, is pleased to
call us an unfortunate people," the letter continued.

> We admit it. We were unfortunate in 1847, through the
> inscrutable ways of God, who however, often chastises in
> love. Twenty years later, we are still unfortunate, for your
> Lordship will not allow us to forget our sad destiny. The
> memory of all past afflictions must be kept fresh, and all
> the charities of which we have been the unfortunate
> recipients must be turned into an argument to force us to
> surrender, in silence, all the advantages of our present
> altered condition, which we owe to our own efforts, under
> the blessing of God and the generous sympathy of our
> immediate pastors. Certainly, we are a peculiar unfortunate
> people.
>   Thousands of our fellow countrymen left their native
> land in 1847 to seek a home in Canada. They did not come
> here to live on charity. They were for the most part in the
> prime of their lives. Their intention was to repay the
> hospitality promised them in this new country by the riches
> of their labour, of their enterprise and of their virtue. God
> willed it otherwise. Your Lordship was our benefactor: we
> always knew it and never failed to acknowledge our
> obligations.

In arguing his case, McGee even threatened violence. "Do not, we pray,
try to force amalgamation upon a people, who, without a single exception,
hold it in horror," he warned. "It cannot succeed. We know ourselves and

we know our neighbours. We assure your lordship, in the presence of God, that an attempt to introduce a double service into Saint Patrick's would likely lead to bloodshed, and consequently to a domestic war between Irish and (French) Canadian Catholics throughout the city. We state this deliberately, not as a menace but as a dutiful warning. We know how far the influence of our priests may go. In this matter it would be powerless."

A petition with 6,000 names was delivered to the bishop's palace. Bourget ignored it. On Christmas Day he sent a second pastoral letter to Saint Patrick's declaring the protest "insufficient." Nothing would prevent Bourget from reducing the territory served by Saint Patrick's (still a branch chapel of Notre Dame) and making it French-speaking. "It is a fact that nobody can deny, that by order of the Sovereign Pontiff, there exists between the bishop and the seminary of St. Sulpice, an arrangement by which the Parish of Notre Dame may be divided at the discretion of the bishop, and that this arrangement has the Pope's approval," Bourget declared. He also ruled out any suggestion of an appeal.

"You cannot appeal to Rome without appealing from the Pope badly informed to the Pope better informed," he reasoned. In other words: *Roma locuta est, causa finita est*—Rome has spoken, and that's the end of it. "You cannot appeal to Rome, because *I* consider it a definite judgment and without appeal. You can not appeal without questioning the Pope's authority itself." The Sulpicians dug in and hired George Etienne Cartier as their lawyer to fight the case. Enough of a strategist to know nothing would be gained from a public fight with his bishop, Father Dowd remained outwardly silent, but he worked behind the scenes to have an appeal filed with the Holy See. He hoped that McGee would do the job. In April 1867 McGee took the temperance pledge and announced he was giving up drinking; at the same time he said he was going to Rome at his own expense to petition the Pope. Although McGee helped draft the constitution that made Canada a country on July 1, 1867, and in spite of his work for the church, he was not popular in his own constituency. Confederation in Canada coincided with a crisis in Ireland and the resurgence of the Fenian movement. McGee attacked the Fenians and urged them to swear allegiance to the Crown saying it was possible for "an Irishman well governed to become one of the best subjects of the Sovereign." In the election of 1867 McGee ran against Bernard Devlin, a criminal lawyer who was also a member of Saint Patrick's. Not only did

Father Dowd endorse McGee, but he also refused absolution to anyone who wouldn't declare themselves politically. Devlin and his supporters especially resented Father Dowd's interference. Many Liberals, including Devlin, transferred to the Gésu where they could confess their sins, not their politics. During the campaign McGee accused several of his opponents of being Fenian sympathisers . He couldn't prove his claims, and the campaign turned ugly. Opinion in the Irish Catholic community was divided. McGee won by a handful of votes but the fight made him a political liability. When the prime minister of the new nation, John A. Macdonald, named his first cabinet, McGee was not included.

Several months later McGee was shot to death on an Ottawa street, thought to be a victim of a Fenian conspiracy. His funeral was held at Saint Patrick's on April 13, 1868, on what would have been his 43rd birthday. It was an historic moment in the life of the infant country. Children were held aloft to see the immense procession of soldiers, horses dressed with head plumes, and the ornate hearse bunted in black. Sixty Protestant clergymen assisted Father Dowd at the requiem mass. The *Montreal Star*, in the overwrought language of the day, described the occasion:

The pulpit, the sanctuary and the altars were hung with black cloth fringed with white. Festoons of black and white stretched from pillar to pillar, while from a suspended crown in the centre of the church sprang, or rather fell, four others. Beneath these a catafalque was erected, surrounded by tapers.

The gallery of the church was crowded with the choir, and the ladies of the congregation. The body of the church is empty, a forest of tapers around the catafalque. The walls of the sanctuary are all ablaze with pictures and natural decorations of oriental warmth and gorgeousness. Above, the Virgin and St. Patrick keep watch in sculptured stone over the praying people beneath. In the sanctuary are ranged white robed priests and acolytes, each with tapers. As each one passes before the great altar which is splendid with gold and silver, though hung with sombre black, the sunlight streams, or rather steals mellowly through the painted palms, dusky with saints and rich with lavish colours, blue,

State Funeral of Thomas D'Arcy McGee
in Montreal, Easter Monday, April 18, 1868.
Looking west on St. Jacques from St. Pierre Street.
Thomas D'Arcy McGee Collection, Concordia University Archives.

crimsons and gold.

The organ peals out its first solemn sounds. The organ seemed to be made for high services under the subdued light of stained glass. Through the doors came the light and the sounds of outer day, the boom of minute guns, the tolling of bells up in windy towers, the tramp of a thousand feet. The coffin is brought in and planted on the threshold. A train of priests move slowly down the central aisle to bid the dead traveller welcome for the last time to the sanctuary where he has knelt so often.

The homily at the funeral was delivered by Father Michael Farrell who not only recounted McGee's contributions to the nation and to the church, but of McGee's triumph over his own failings. "He had his faults, everyone knows, but towards the end there had been a change," said Farrell "This change might be seen in the (temperance) resolution which he kept so inviolably until the day of his death, to abstain from those social excesses which could mar so considerably the effect of his talents. Let those who are as tempted as he was, appreciate the amount of self-sacrifice which such a resolution involves."

The location of McGee's pew on the left-hand side of the main aisle, number 240, is today identified by a maple leaf flag. However the precise historic pew he occupied was lost in the shuffle by careless workmen during renovations to the church in 1992. Three rows behind, on the right-hand side of the church is another pew of interest, although it is not identified. It was once where James Whelan, the man convicted and hanged for McGee's assassination, knelt to pray. Whelan was married in Saint Patrick's in February 1867; his wife, Bridgit Doyle ran a boarding house near the church on St. Alexandre Street. She never believed her husband guilty, and on every anniversary of his execution, she displayed his picture in a mourning wreath in her window. Dowd asked her to stop the practice, and she complied. She remained a faithful parishioner. Every morning until she died in November 1904, she attended the 7 a.m. mass dressed in a black bonnet with a black mourning veil, and she showed up each year at the strawberry social.

The stalemate between Dowd and Bishop Bourget over the future of

Saint Patrick's dragged on. An Irish priest, M.B. Buckley, who came to Montreal in 1870 to raise money for a cathedral in Cork, detected the animosity. "A great antipathy seems to exist between the French and the Irish, clearly not on religious grounds, inasmuch as both are Catholics; but the feeling illustrates the truth that men's minds are embittered as much, if not more, by political and national prejudices as by difference of religious faith," Buckley wrote in his diary. "In many places efforts have been made by the ecclesiastical authorities to blend the two nationalities, but oil and water are not more dissociable. Not only here, but elsewhere I have remarked that there is a decided prejudice against Irish Catholics, and that it is only by some fortunate combination of circumstances, or by the force of rare talent that such a one can attain in the States or Canada any prominent position."

In August 1870 Bishop Bourget launched a pre-emptive strike when he laid the cornerstone for Montreal's new cathedral two blocks west of Saint Patrick's. Conceived as a replica of St. Peter's in Rome, the cathedral's location in the heart of Montreal's English-speaking district was a strategic manoeuvre to upstage the Sulpicians and to admonish everyone that Bourget's would be the "overpowering voice which continually speaks to the diocese, reminding them that their faith is the faith of Rome." As a political statement the building offers magnificent insight into 19th-century Quebec nationalism and Roman Catholicism. Shortly before the foundation for the cathedral was laid, the newspaper *L'Opinion* reported that it would be "Roman, pure and simple." At the time Pope Pius IX was under attack in Garibaldi's fight to unify Italy. In 1870 the pontiff was stripped of his temporal powers, and as an expression of solidarity Bourget ordered a great new church built in the Italian Renaissance style. If the Pope could not be king of Rome, Bourget would reproduce Rome for the Pope in Montreal.

Whatever claims Saint Patrick's thought it might have to its parish boundaries appeared to have been set back in 1871 when the Vatican Council reinforced the notion of papal primacy and infallibility. Dowd's task was made even more difficult. He now had to oppose Bourget without being insubordinate, and he had to frustrate the bishop's designs on Saint Patrick's without being rebellious. The city looked on and awaited the outcome of the dispute between the bishop and his pastor. A final day of reckoning was imminent.

To the relief of those who preferred a negotiated diplomatic solution to the impasse, Rome invited Archbishop Elzéar Alexandre Taschereau of Quebec City to mediate. Taschereau, who would later become Canada's first cardinal, was a realist, a moderate and a progressive Catholic with a reputation as a conciliator. Although he took pride in being objective, he disdained ultramontasist thinking and therefore from the outset was biased against Bourget. In his dispatches to Rome, Taschereau discredited Bourget as a lightweight. One year later, the Vatican ruled. The bad news was that the Sulpicians would lose Saint Patrick's and be required to turn it over to the diocese. The good news was that the parish boundaries would be undisturbed and continue to "cover one and the same territory in such a way that the French-speaking Catholics are subject to the pastor of the Mother Church, Notre Dame, and the Angli, or Hibernenses living in the same territory are subject to the pastor of Saint Patrick's. *Roma locuta est: causa finita est.*"

Rome had indeed spoken. Bourget was forced to annul his decree.

It was a triumph for common sense, but ultimately a costly one. The precedent would lead to the duplication of English and French facilities in almost every area. The most obvious examples are in Point St. Charles, where two churches, St. Gabriel's and St. Charles, were built beside each other on Centre Street; in Westmount, where St. Leon's and the Church of the Ascension occupy the same block, and in N.D.G. where St. Augustine's and Notre Dame de Grace are a five minute walk apart. At the same time Saint Patrick's was designated both a national and a territorial parish, both a mother church for all English-speaking Catholics on the island of Montreal, and as a parish home for those within its geographical boundaries.

Even though the dispute had been resolved it was not the end of Saint Patrick's burdens. There was still $300,000 owing on the church and the Sulpicians, good businessmen that they are, expected to be paid for the building. The parishioners of Saint Patrick's would be required to buy it. Of the outstanding bill $278,000 carried interest of four and a half percent. The remaining $22,000 was an interest-free loan from the seminary which the Sulpicians were willing to forgive. But until the rest of the debt was retired, the wardens of Notre Dame would continue to conduct the affairs of Saint Patrick's .

Chapter Six

THE COMMUNITY HAILED Father Dowd as a hero, as the tenacious priest who saved Saint Patrick's, and as a result his grip on the parish was unassailable He was strict but straightforward, and historian Loye tells us he was "prone to anger at times, and could be vindictive where his legitimate authority or political opinion was questioned." Anyone who crossed him had their knuckles rapped. Dowd's blunt words and sometimes tactless behaviour were, however, tempered by his extraordinary ability to charm. Still, anyone who challenged him did so at their peril. Once when a newcomer from Boston, Larry Gouverny, publicly suggested that the 1874 St. Patrick's Day parade be cancelled and that the money for the procession be sent instead to relieve the starving in Ireland, Dowd ridiculed the idea from the pulpit. "Can you conceive of a more despicable animal than a Yankeefied Irishman?" he snapped. The most notorious incident, however, was the result of Dowd's ongoing feud with the president of the St. Patrick's Society, Dr. Barney Devlin. Devlin, a Liberal, had opposed McGee in Montreal West in the 1867 election, and came within a handful of votes of defeating him. In 1875 Devlin was elected member for Montreal Centre by acclamation and decided his authority as an MP and as president of the patriotic St. Patrick's Society easily matched Dowd's. Dowd had always mistrusted Devlin; he suspected him of being a Fenian. A clash between the two men was inevitable. The incident that set off their celebrated public quarrel began on December 4, 1875 when two priests, James Murphy, one of Saint Patrick's curates, and Daniel Lynch, a visiting priest from Newfoundland, died in a fire at Sault-au-Recollect. The priests were on their way to visit a mutual friend in St. Adele and stopped at a hotel that caught fire. The two men were trapped in the burning building. Thousands turned out for their funeral at Saint Patrick's five days later. It was by all accounts an especially emotional event in the life of the community. "Strong men who had seen death in many forms, tender sympathetic women and children gave vent to their feelings in plenteous weeping," read one newspaper story, "and still from the roof loft came the agonising strains of the organ, low, soft, plaintive, stealing through the aisles and into the hearts of the surrounding people below, fading away into the draperies of desolation, and again recurring as if the soul of a great woe were being poured through the pipes of the mighty instrument." However, the bells of Saint Patrick's weren't tolled at the funeral, and Devlin took umbrage at what he considered a breach in protocol. The next day Devlin wrote an open letter to the *Gazette* in which he accused Father Dowd of "insulting the Irish Catholics of the Dominion by an apparently premeditated and wilful omission to toll the funeral bells of the Catholic churches of this city, an omission considered the more galling owing to its never having occurred before upon such a solemn occasion, and whereas our national self-assertion and the preservation of the respect we owe to our church demand an explanation of this strange and painful circumstance, I hereby convene a special meeting of the St. Patrick's Society."

Two days later, on Sunday, December 12, Dowd was in the pulpit with a copy of the newspaper under his arm. His sermon began quietly enough. "Before I make any particular remarks, I would explain to all of you the rules which govern the ringing of the bells," he said patiently. "The bishop is the only one who has a right to order of a general ringing of the bells of the Catholic churches of the city.

"I am now in my twenty-eighth year of priesthood and there is only one single instance in my memory where the ecclesiastical authorities thought it proper to have all the bells rung, and that was on the occasion of the death of poor Mr. McGee. This occasion I believe could not be taken as a precedent for any other one. It was a public funeral conducted by the government, and all Catholics and Protestants united in prayer against the horrid crime."

Then whacking the newspaper on the railing, he launched into an unprecedented attack on Devlin who was seated directly below. Branding him a man of "hellish principle, determined to trample on the rights of the church," he accused Devlin of "threatening the peace of our Catholic body in Montreal with division and rancour.

"Was I asked to ring the bells? Did anyone hint to me it would be advisable to do so?" Dowd roared. "I am charged with insulting because I did not think of doing what nobody else thought of doing. No person thought it desirable that they should be rung, and yet this omission was a deliberate disrespect of the memory of the departed priests.

"Who asked for an explanation? Did the humblest member of the congregation or any other come to me? I did not care if only a little child came, I would have given an explanation. I hold no one responsible for this but the person over whose signature it stands. Did Devlin come to me? No!"

Dowd had spoken; Devlin was discredited.

Antagonism between the two surfaced again three years later when Devlin sought re-election. Dowd campaigned openly against him. "Mackenzie's (Liberal) government is rotten to the core," Dowd told anyone who would listen, "and Devlin is part of it." Devlin was defeated.[*]

Bishop Bourget resigned as bishop of Montreal in September 1876, and was succeeded by Edouard Charles Fabre. Fabre was more liberal than his predecessor and sought accommodation rather than confrontation. He did, however, introduce new levies on every Catholic in the diocese to pay for the cathedral which was still under construction. Father Dowd, still saddled with the mortgage on Saint Patrick's, resented having to shoulder part of the debt for an oversized cathedral that everyone feared would become a white elephant.

In the spring of 1877 Dowd led a pilgrimage of 75 parishioners rich enough to pay the $300 fare in gold to Rome to take part in celebrations marking the 50th anniversary of Pope Pius IX's consecration as a bishop. Dowd's thoughts as he left on the voyage were of death. "I resolve in my innermost soul to devote myself to the end of my days with renewed zeal and fidelity to the service of people of whom I know I am unworthy," he told a send-off gathering. "This I know, is the resolution of an old man, and it supposes that 'ere very long you shall have the trouble of burying me. I was ordained not for myself, but to do the work of God, and that wherever he pleased to call me. He pleased to call me to Montreal. I simply did my

---

[*] Devlin died in Colorado, in February 1880, eighteen months after his last campaign. His body was brought back to Montreal. At Devlin's funeral in Saint Patrick's, Father Dowd described his nemesis as "a man who could create bitter enemy as well as warm friend, but," he said, "on this occasion I will forget the bitterness of the violent contests of the past."

duty by obeying. And what have I lost? Do I not find in this Saint Patrick's of ours the same peace and happiness, the same confidence and friendship, the same obedience and generous charity, the same warm Irish hearts that I left in the old land?"

The pilgrims set sail from New York on April 21, aboard the Inman liner *City of Brussels*. The ship was supposed arrive in Southampton May 1, but was overdue, first by one day, then by one week. Telegraphy didn't exist and there was no method of ship-to-shore communication. By May 9 everyone feared the worst. "Despite the confidence which the agents of the Inman line have sought to infuse into the minds of those interested in the safety of the *City of Brussels*, it cannot now be concealed that much and painful anxiety exists as to the whereabouts of the pilgrimage ship," stated the *Gazette*. By the second weekend of May it was presumed the ship was lost. Prayers were offered for the missing travellers in all churches throughout the city, regardless of denomination. On Sunday May 13, high mass at Saint Patrick's was interrupted with the news that the *City of Brussels* had been found. Three days out of New York the vessel had lost a propeller shaft and rather than return for repairs the passengers voted to proceed to Europe under sail. They were at sea for five weeks and two days before they arrived in Liverpool. Although they missed the pope's jubilee celebrations, they went on to Paris, Lourdes, and Bordeaux, then to Rome on June 15 for an audience with the 88-year-old pontiff. A Vatican dispatch records that Father Dowd gave the Pope "a magnificent miter studded with gems, a silver vase, and $20,000 in cash." The pope expressed joy at the escape of the pilgrims from the great perils of their voyage, and presented Dowd with a gold fountain pen. Dowd spent a month in Ireland on an ancestral visit before returning to a volatile situation in Montreal on August 13. On July 12 during a King Billy Parade there had been a clash in Victoria Square between Irish Catholics and Protestants in which a young Protestant, Thomas Lett Hackett, had been shot and killed. The press held the Roman Catholics liable for Hackett's death. Catholics claimed the Orangemen provoked the incident and promised to march again "knee deep in blood if need be." In his first sermon upon his return to Saint Patrick's Dowd was conciliatory and pledged to "expel from the hitherto happy city of Montreal the demon of discord.

"Only a few weeks before that unhappy 12th of July all were at peace," he said. "Catholics and Protestants vied with one another for the prosperity of our city and in acts of mutual kindness and brotherhood." As an example he cited the prayers that been offered in all the churches of the city for his safe return.

> A number of Catholic pilgrims were exposed to the perils of the ocean and it was feared they were lost. The big, kind hearts of Montreal were moved to the extreme. Protestant vied with Catholic in sympathy and in anxiety, and when the good news of safety arrived, the vaults of Saint Patrick's did not resound with less praise and thanksgiving to God than did that of the Protestant churches of this city.

> What demon came amongst us to efface this beautiful picture? The evil genius of Orangeism must have a new triumph over Catholic following, Catholic honour and Catholic faith in the streets of Montreal. To this all must be sacrificed—the peace of our city, its good name, its perspicacity, and the union and happiness of its inhabitants. Will the citizens of Montreal again permit this crime against their city and against themselves? If I know them, they will not.

Dowd used his extraordinary skills as a conciliator to work with the Protestant clergy to defuse what could have become a bitter, prolonged religious feud. He had a network of friends among the Protestant clergy, and now was able to draw from a reserve of ecumenical goodwill that he had built up within the community. When the Unitarian church burned, it was Dowd who had provided accommodation for the congregation in Saint Patrick's hall; he had taken in Irish Protestant orphans and waived the rules so they weren't required to be educated as Catholics, and he had worked with Anglicans to provide help for the poor in their parishes.

Genuinely pleased to have their pastor back in the pulpit, the congregation presented Dowd with a life-sized portrait of himself at a banquet in September. Dowd seemed to be genuinely embarrassed by gifts, and often sold anything of value and turned the proceeds over to charity or to the fabrique to reduce the mortgage on the church, but the portrait he kept.[*] By now, Dowd was more than accustomed to the rhythms of his diocese. Saint Patrick's was becoming recognised as the heart of a prosperous lace-curtain uptown Irish neighbourhood known as "Little Dublin," far removed from the so-called "shanty Irish" attached to St. Ann's in Griffintown. Father Buckley, the visiting priest from Ireland, gives us a glimpse of life in Dowd's rectory. "The rules of the house are new to us," Buckley wrote "They rise at 4:30 a.m., breakfast *ad libitum*, dine at 11:30 and supper at 7. Night prayers at 8:30 and after that, bed. I agree to conform to all except the early rising, but I learn that I am not bound to observe any part of the rule; but am perfectly free to act as I please. I do conform, however, through respect." During his three weeks in Montreal Buckley proved to be an eager tourist, and went to see "four churches, each of a different religion. It appears the people here are very church going, and on Sunday it was easy to observe that this was true, for the streets were utterly deserted up to two o'clock in the afternoon," he wrote.

> Saint Patrick's Church, where the Irish most do congregate, is a splendid Gothic structure, quite finished and well situated. The spire, however, is too small in proportion to the tower, and does not look well, being covered with tin instead of slate; and here I may remark that tin roofing is very general in Canada. It keeps its colour well and is lasting.

One visitor, who sat in the church for two hours to get a good seat for the mass on St. Patrick's Day in the 1870's, found that was "ample time to study and enjoy the scene that the church decorations presented" and was impressed by the "simple elegance about the arrangements of the altar and the lights and the shades of the sanctuary ... at various points were suspended flags of different colours, the whole blending to form a picture worthy of an artist. At intervals, on the pillars in the body of the church ornamental shields were hung on which mottos of scripture and national import were emblazoned in striking characters."

The Irish, who constituted the pariah class when they first arrived depended on the church to lead them up and out. A visiting Irish MP in the

---

[*]The painting seems to have disappeared. There is no trace of it either in the church, the rectory, or the current Father Dowd home.

British House of Commons, John Francis McGuire, noted in his diary "the influence of really good priests in Montreal who lift the Irish up, raise their social position, induce them to acquire and to accumulate property and to identify themselves with the progress of the community." As the Irish grew in numbers, they grew in strength, and by 1873 had enough political clout to elect a Liberal lawyer, Francis Cassidy, the first Irish Catholic mayor of Montreal.* Cassidy died within three months of taking office, but two years later another Irish Catholic, Dr. William Hales Hingston, professor of clinical surgery at Hôtel Dieu Hospital, was elected mayor. Hingston was the son of an Irish half-pay officer who had come to Canada with his regiment in 1805. Dr. Hingston's election was exemplary, proof that given the opportunity, children and grandchildren of Irish immigrants could make their way out of the ghetto in the City Below the Hill up into the Square Mile and take their place among the ranks of the city's ruling class. One of Quebec's most famous tragic poets, Émile Nelligan** was baptised in Saint Patrick's on Christmas Day 1879. The story of how his mother, afraid her sickly child would die, bundled him up and brought him to the church in the dead of night to be baptised, has become folklore. Nelligan started writing poetry in French when he was 17, and for the next two years astonished everyone with his verse. His editor, Louis Dantin, wrote of him, "Born of an Irish father and a French Canadian mother, he felt boiling within him the mixture of these two generous bloodlines. He had the intelligence, quickness, the devilish impetuosity of the Gallic race, exasperated by the dreamy mysticism and the dark melancholy of a Celtic bard."

Nelligan represented the third generation of Montreal Irish. By 1879 the 4,000 survivors of Black '47 who remained in Montreal had doubled the city's Irish population. Dowd had baptised many of them as infants, married them, then baptised their children. His overriding concern was with the welfare of children. One story in Edgar Andrew Collard's Montreal *Gazette* series "All Our Yesterdays" illustrates how much Dowd was respected as a social worker. A nine-year old waif was picked up for vagrancy and hauled into court for questioning. As soon as the presiding judge established

---

*John Easton Mills, elected mayor by council in 1846, and William Workman, elected mayor in 1868 were both of Irish Protestant descent.
**Nelligan had a mental breakdown in 1899 and never wrote again. He was confined to a mental hospital where he died on November 18, 1941.

that the child was a Roman Catholic and had no home "his honour thought it best to send him to Father Dowd who would look after him accordingly." It was a rather routine occurrence, Collard writes, "Send them to Father Dowd, he'll look after them. And he did." Dowd saw himself as the shepherd of his flock, preferring to cajole rather than to scold to keep it in line. The two celebrations he most enjoyed were St. Patrick's Day and the feast of Corpus Christi. On those two occasions he spared no expense to decorate the church. The *Star's* description of the St. Patrick's Day Parade from Victoria Square up Beaver Hall Hill to the church in 1885 is typical: "The interior of Saint Patrick's church was simply decorated with streamers in red, white, and green flannel, suspended from the ceiling, bannerets and flags bearing shamrocks, harps ,and appropriate mottos hung from the pillars, and shields bearing various devices graced the gallery front and chancel. The altar was profuse with flowers in green and white, and a large illuminated harp and Irish cross stood at either side." Archbishop Fabre celebrated the mass, and Toronto's Bishop Mahoney O'Mahoney preached the sermon. Martial music wafted into the building from the bands outside which, according to one account, "seemed to be playing for dear life. The blending of the music was hardly as harmonious as it might have been." The presence of the military bands was prescient. Two weeks later word of the Duck Lake Massacre in the North West Territories reached Montreal; the Riel Rebellion had begun. The Métis, who made up a majority of the population in the west, tired of having their legitimate grievances ignored by the government in Ottawa, established a provisional government of their own. Riel, their messianic, troubled leader, issued an ultimatum, ordering the Canadian authorities out of the west. When they refused to leave, Riel's guerrillas ambushed a Mounted Police contingent at Duck Lake, killing 12. Troops from Montreal left for the West in April, and the uprising was crushed in May. Riel surrendered.

Far more calamitous for Montreal than the political situation in the west was the smallpox epidemic that began in the city that spring. Former mayor Hingston, a member of the board of health, immediately alerted Dowd to the danger. Dowd had never forgotten the impact of the deadly typhus epidemic and heeded Hingston's advice that the church set up a clinic where members of the congregation could be vaccinated. By the end of May more than 800 of Saint Patrick's parishioners were immunised.

French diocesan priests, wary of the procedure, were not as forceful. In early June after the Corpus Christi procession the contagion spread. By July the city was in the grip of the red death. On August 18 one of the city's most prominent residents, former prime minister of the United Canadian Provinces and elder statesman, Sir Francis Hincks died. His body was immediately buried in the dead of night.

Protestants in the city suggested French Roman Catholics were responsible for spreading the disease. The Board of Health introduced compulsory vaccination, and an urban myth spread through French parts of Montreal that vaccination was somehow an English plot to infect French-speaking Quebecers. One newspaper, *La Patrie*, went so far as to claim the "English were intent on genocide." The ignorance proved costly. Montreal reported the highest mortality rate in the country, 33 deaths per 1,000 population. Returns from the health office revealed that of the 3,000 victims of the disease, 91 percent were French-speaking. In an effort to curb the spread of the disease the Board of Trade wanted close all public buildings where crowds gathered, including the churches. Bishop Fabre wouldn't hear of it. "To close the churches would simply be to laugh at God, to go against His wishes," he countered. "No, let the churches remain open." Fabre instead invoked the intercession of St. Roch, the patron saint of plague victims, and on Sunday, November 1, All Soul's Day, Father Dowd offered a special mass at Saint Patrick's "for the cessation of the smallpox."

As the epidemic raged, throngs crowded public demonstrations held in Montreal in support of Louis Riel. Riel had surrendered in May and was charged with treason. He was put on trial in Regina, found guilty and sentenced to hang. In Quebec, Riel's guilt or innocence was incidental to the popular view that he had not received a fair trial, that only six men sat on the jury, and that he had been condemned by an English judge, not because he had led a rebellion, but because he was French-speaking. Agitation mounted in Quebec as the government postponed the execution three times. Early in November Dowd sent a letter to Prime Minister John A. Macdonald counselling prudence in the Riel affair. Dowd did not advocate clemency outright, but expressed "extreme doubt that the penalty would be carried out." If Riel were to be hanged, Dowd warned, the execution would "be a cause of future recrimination and discord." Riel was executed on November 16, and on November 22, one of the greatest mass meetings ever held in Montreal took place when 30,000 people jammed the Champs de Mars to enshrine Riel in Quebec consciousness as a martyred hero. The mass meeting did not, as feared, inflame the smallpox epidemic. With the onset of winter, the plague ended.

Father Dowd celebrated the fiftieth anniversary of his ordination on May 19, 1887. By then he was so well known that one letter addressed simply to "Father Dowd, America," was delivered to him. To mark the anniversary a huge hand-lettered banner unfurled across the street near the church proclaimed "We Thank God for Our Pastor's Jubilee and Welcome and Honour It." All of the city's newspapers urged "every friend of Father Dowd's should wear a jubilee badge. The badge is a most handsome one and will make an appropriate bookmark after its use." Three arch-bishops, two bishops and 50 priests celebrated the golden jubilee mass. According to the *Gazette* the event was "one of indescribable beauty, the sanctuary was brilliantly decorated with flags, banners, and bannerets bearing appropriate mottos and insignia while the small altars and statues were beautifully decked with flowers of various hues and lit up with lamps of many colours. On the gospel side was a throne erected for the archbishop, and the clergy who assisted at the mass, occupied raised seats on either side of the sanctuary."

At a banquet afterwards* the Grand Old Man was given a "a pinch of snuff in a very pretty floral box," a gold chalice, and a cheque for $22,000. The well-known Montreal photographer William Notman took a picture. Dowd kept the snuff and the Notman photograph, but signed the cheque over to reduce the church debt, and gave the chalice to the church. "It is not the little good I've done that troubles me," he said, "but I am often troubled by the thought of the good I have left undone."

Obviously touched by the homage, Dowd grew sentimental. "All my faults have disappeared, and the little good I have done has grown into such proportions that I must look at it twice before I recognise it as my own," he told the assembled guests. "Behind, and not far behind your kindness, I see the judgment of another tribunal. Before long I will have to stand and answer to an all-seeing and all-knowing God, and you my friends will not be there to excuse my failings."

---

*The honours were shared with Rev. Joseph Toupin, a curate at the church, who was Dowd's right-hand from 1854 until his death in 1896.

Dowd had neglected material comfort during his years as pastor but finally recognised the need for a church presbytery to house the curates. Designed by Montreal architect William Edward Doran, and built at a cost of $20,000, it opened in 1887. "It is a handsome stone house, three stories in height with a mansard roof and is about 50 feet in length by 40 in width," The *Catholic Weekly Review* reported.

> The entrance door is broad and massive. To the right of the entrance hall is the porter's room and beyond it the office of the Rev. Father Dowd, fitted with an iron safe wherein the parish records are to be deposited. At the further end of the corridor is the Archbishop's suite of apartments. One end of the corridor terminates in a staircase of the ordinary pattern; at the other end is a wonderful spiral affair in wrought iron which twists through the entire height of the house. On the second flat are the bedroom and the study of the Rev. Father Dowd. The view from these apartments is very pleasant giving on the north the mountain and some intervening gardens. Some of the assistant priests will be established on this flat and others on the flat above where there is a large library and seven bedrooms. Each priest will have a study or sitting room leading from his sleeping apartment. In the basement are the refectory, with its adjacent pantries, the kitchen, the storerooms, etc. There are four exits to the house, one from the basement, one leading to the residence of the caretaker of the church, one on Dorchester St. and one to a passage connecting with Saint Patrick's church. The new presbytery, though not large is well planned and prettily built. It reflects credit on the architect and also on St. Patrick's congregation for having provided so handsome a house for their devoted pastors.

One of Father Dowd's closest companions in his declining years was Rev. Edmund Wood, the Anglican rector and founding pastor of St. John the Evangelist Church on Ontario Street. In spite of their denominational differences, the two men had great affinity. Both were mavericks, both ministered to the poor, and Wood, a High Anglican, had clashed with his bishop over the use of Roman Catholic rituals in his service. Wood often joined Dowd for dinner at the rectory. Dowd's table was filled with simple but abundant fare, usually potatoes and overcooked beef. As one dinner guest diplomatically put it, "the best sauces served at the table were Father Dowd's fatherly smiles and pleasing anecdotes." Dowd smoked a pipe, used snuff, liked cigars, and enjoyed the occasional glass of whisky. Even as he grew older, his daily routine never changed.

On February 2, 1891, another of Saint Patrick's most prominent parishioners, James McShane, was elected mayor of Montreal. McShane, a butcher's son, grew up in Griffintown and became a stockbroker. He was elected to the provincial legislature in 1873, and served as minister of agriculture and public works in the cabinet of Premier Honoré Mercier. Other Irishmen had served in political office, but none was as popular or as much of a populist as "The People's Jimmy" McShane. The impact of his election in the Irish community and the prestige for the church cannot be underestimated. On St. Patrick's Day, 1891, Father Dowd announced as his "final work before leaving on my grand journey," plans to decorate the interior of Saint Patrick's. Church revenues had steadily increased and the mortgage would be paid off within ten years. The time was opportune to refurbish the interior in time for the golden jubilee in 1897. William Doran was engaged as the architect, but Father Dowd never lived to see the work completed. Early in December he developed pneumonia. When a priest gave him the last rites, Dowd brushed him aside. "I don't feel sick, but I guess my opinion doesn't count for much." They were his last words. He died one week before Christmas at the age of 77.

"It would have been a touching sermon to have visited his room and his wardrobe after his death, to have seen the fewness, the primitiveness of the wants of this man," said one of his curates. "With the exception of an armchair which a gentleman of the parish gave him when he was ill with rheumatism, I don't think the effects of his room if sold at auction would realise ten dollars." More than a beloved priest, Dowd had become an institution and most of his parishioners thought of him as permanent. His obituary in the *Herald* ran under the sub heading: "Let His Good Deeds be Engraved in Brass and his Failings Written on Water." In an unprecedented display of respect for a clergyman, city council postponed its meeting, citing "the calamity that has befallen the Irish Catholic community." Flags throughout Montreal were lowered to half-mast. Dowd's coffin was laid out not in Saint Patrick's but in the parish church, Notre Dame, and an endless line of people, including the Anglican Bishop of Montreal, William Bennett Bond, filed past to pay their respects. If the newspapers' estimates are to be believed, 20,000, or two-thirds of Montreal's population turned out.

According to the account in the Montreal *Star,*

> The congregation, as they came silently into the church gazed with love and sorrow intermingled at the remains of the man who had for many years shared and counselled them in times of sorrow and trouble. Father Dowd is now but a memory, never, indeed to be erased while Saint Patrick's exists.

Church bells throughout the city tolled as his funeral cortege made its way through the snow to the Grand Seminary on Sherbooke Street, where he was buried.* As a final epitaph, the Montreal *Gazette* recalled his enormous contributions as a social worker. "School, refuge and asylum are the monuments of his holy zeal. It can be said of him in truth that 'his bones, when he has run his course and sleeps in blessing, will have a tomb of orphans' tears wept on them.'"

---

*Father Dowd's remains were exhumed in 1982 and reinterred in a vault on the south-east wall of the Grand Seminary's crypt.

Chapter Seven

FATHER DOWD was succeeded by his second-in-command, John Joseph Patrick Quinlivan, the first native-born Canadian to take charge of Saint Patrick's. Quinlivan came from Stratford, Ontario where he was born on September 17, 1846. He studied classics with the Basilians in Toronto, then went to Paris where he took his theology and joined the Gentlemen of St. Sulpice. He arrived in Montreal in 1876 to teach at the Grand Seminary and was ordained there on September 28, 1878. Soon thereafter he was assigned as a curate to Saint Patrick's. Within weeks Quinlivan's diligence saved the church a fortune, and in the process, Father Dowd from embarrassment. As a result he quickly became Father Dowd's most trusted advisor. A story related by Edgar Andrew Collard explains why. In 1869 Father Dowd had used money from the estate of the wealthy Irishman Bartholomew O'Brien to build and to maintain St. Bridgit's refuge. Twenty years after the home was built, one of O'Brien's close relatives arrived in Montreal demanding a share of the estate. Father Dowd had been one of three executors of O'Brien's will and was certain the relative had been paid whatever inheritance was due. But, Collard writes, Dowd had lost the receipt from the legatee, and could not prove it.

Though Father Dowd searched high and low he could not find what had happened to it. During the long interval since the will was settled, the other two executors who acted with him had died. Father Dowd had no means of meeting the legatee's demands except by paying him out of the funds O'Brien had earmarked for St. Bridgit's. The loss of the money might imperil the future of the institution.

Archbishop Fabre consulted experts in Rome. He was advised that that if the case went to court, judgment would be found against Father Dowd. If there was a receipt, Father

Quinlivan was determined to find it. He rummaged through everything until he found an enormous tin box covered with dust. It was full of old documents, many discoloured by time. None of them seemed relevant. They concerned another institution, Saint Patrick's orphanage. Father Quinlivan, however, would not give up. He unfolded and examined every document. In the end nothing remained but a couple of nondescript papers at the bottom of the box. He unfolded the last of them. It was the missing receipt. He looked at his watch. It was dinnertime. Father Dowd would be coming to dine with his curates. Father Quinlivan hurried into the dining room flourishing the receipt.

It was, Collard assures us, "the happiest, most cheerful dinner the clergy of Saint Patrick's ever enjoyed." So when Dowd died Quinlivan's appointment as his successor came as no great surprise. "He is a thoroughly educated gentleman of a rather retiring disposition," the *Star* observed. "He is a quick student, an indefatigable worker, and an easy but convincing speaker. He is a man worthy of the greatest confidences. He fully appreciates the sterling qualities of his predecessor, so no doubt he will walk closely in his footsteps." The *Herald* was less diplomatic about Quinlivan's skill in the pulpit. "A pleasing, though by no means an eloquent preacher, his sermons for the most part are simple," it reported. Still, Quinlivan, everyone agreed, was a superb administrator and an efficient business manager. It was, incidentally, through Quinlivan that French-Canadians were introduced to professional hockey. At the end of the 19th century the old-monied Protestant families considered Irish Catholics second-class citizens. Athletic clubs in the city were segregated. Catholics, for example, weren't permitted to play for the Montreal Victorias, the Winged Wheelers, or the Wanderers. Saint Patrick's had a lacrosse team of its own that went to the Chicago World's Fair in 1892. When it returned, Quinlivan decided the church should help finance a hockey team for Catholic boys. It was called the Shamrocks. The Irish players on the team proved less than adequate, so French-Canadian Catholics were recruited to play. To everyone's surprise, the team won the Stanley Cup in 1898 and 1899. It has often been argued that French-Canadian hockey supremacy "was nurtured in a field of Irish Shamrocks."

It was left to Quinlivan to carry out Dowd's plan to refurbish the church. First, the tin roof was replaced with slate and the steeple clad in copper. Westmount architect Edward Doran was hired to do the renovations and an interior decorator from Brooklyn, Alexander Locke, the nephew of the apostolic delegate to Canada, Bishop George Conroy, was subcontracted to do the interior decoration. Locke had studied with John Lafarge, who had been associated with the Tiffany Glass Co. He was also responsible for the decoration of Queen of All Saints, St. Joseph's, and St. Augustine's churches in Brooklyn. The contract signed in October 1894 specified that Locke "shall employ the best workers, and if any employed should render themselves objectionable to the Reverend Pastor, they must be withdrawn." Locke was paid $7,800 for the work, but the cost-concious Quinlivan made certain "no gold, bronze or tarnishable metal is to be used, but where gold is required the effect is to be gotten with aluminium leaf lacquered to represent gold." The walls were to be painted in "a quiet salmon tone with just enough body to it to show off ornament in different tones of ivory."

To help finance the decoration Quinlivan held a sale of church property. He sold the pine pews installed in 1861 and even attempted to sell the four Grey Nun windows in the apse behind the altar for $100 each. He took out a newspaper advertisement which read:

> Stained Glass Windows, For Sale Cheap: Four large, rich stained glass windows which do not harmonise with the others are for sale, cheap. The pattern is such that they could easily be divided into eight windows, each about 20 feet in height and about five feet in width. May be had after a month's notice.*

Locke's first decorative contributions were the two immense if somewhat mediocre paintings over the stalls on either side of the sanctuary, one of the Ascension, the other a copy of Titian's "Assumption of the Blessed Virgin." The gold Venetian mosaic Locke designed for the walls of the

*He wasn't able to get rid of them, and when the four new evangelist windows were installed, the lower portion of the Grey Nuns' windows were simply boarded up. They were discovered by accident in 1991 during renovations to the church.

Father Dowd was succeeded by his second-in-command,
John Joseph Quinlivan, the first native-born Canadian to take charge
of Saint Patrick's.
Courtesy of Saint Patrick's Basilica.

sanctuary was inspired by the decoration of St. Mark's in Venice. In the arch of the vault over the high altar appear the arms of Pope Leo XIII and, to reflect the new shared order, on either side appear the arms of Montreal's archbishop, Louis-Joseph Bruchési and of those of the Sulpicians. When the scaffolding came down at the end of April, the *Montreal Star* reported that the church had been "vastly altered and improved.

"The walls have assumed a pleasant terra cotta colour, which is further relieved by groups of fleur de lys and shamrocks painted in delicate shades of cream."The paper also reported that a high altar of white marble would be installed, "with a sculptured canopy of the same material over thirty feet in height. The altar will be erected in the centre of the sanctuary and will allow of a large passage in the rear. A new communion rail of white marble, and stalls and choir seats of oak are to be added, while another marked feature will be the handsome slated floor. The chancel decorations will cost about $25,000 while the total amount expended is expected to reach the sum of $40,000." Plans for the high altar of marble and the communion rail were, however, scrapped because it was felt the decoration would be not only too expensive, but pretentious. wainscotting was added throughout the summer.

Meanwhile, the cathedral up the street which had taken 24 years to build had finally opened on Easter Sunday 1894, and as work began on the renovations to Saint Patrick's there was widespread press speculation that a number of Saint Patrick's prominent pew holders were going to abandon the church and take up pews in the new cathedral two blocks west. Quinlivan denied the rumours. "I have never heard that any of our pew holders were to leave for the Cathedral; on the contrary, we have 389 pews and we are to have 50 more in a few days in the gallery. This will give seating accommodation for 200 more people," he told reporters in May. The gallery or double loft designed by Doran was described in the *True Witness and Catholic Chronicle:*

> The lower, or old gallery, will be fitted up in an amphitheatre form with graded pews and perhaps the best view in the whole church will be had from that section of the edifice. It is surprising, but nevertheless it is a fact that very many good-sized churches do not afford more room

than will the gallery when completed. It is 50 feet deep and 100 feet long. Just imagine a space of 50x100 feet being added thus to Saint Patrick's Church. And yet this change will not necessitate any encroachment upon the space heretofore enjoyed. Seen from the body of the church, this gallery will present a wonderfully grand appearance. The two magnificent elegantly curved staircases that are to lead up to the gallery will form a contrast with the present difficult and corkscrew mode of ascent. Harmony of colouring, fresh floods of light from the unobstructed central window, new space even equivalent to that of a whole church, easy access to the gallery, a magnificent new organ provided with all the modern improvements known to the builders of those instruments, and finally a perfection of design that will stand as an immortalising monument to the genius of the architect.

Locke designed four exquisite stained glass windows depicting the evangelists for the sanctuary: St. Matthew in shades of green, St. Mark in red and purple, St. Luke in yellow and violet, and St. John in ruby and olive. Four much larger windows were imported from Tiroler Glasmalerei in Austria for the nave. The original organ—a three manual instrument with 31 stops built by Samuel Russell Warren in 1852—was split in two so the Catherine wheel window in the church tower could be reopened to the morning sun. Casavant Frères Ltée built a 2,500 pipe organ, but it took several months before it was fully operational. Frederick Archer, a British musician who made his reputation as an organist with the Church of the Incarnation in New York and as the conductor of the Pittsburgh Symphony, formally inaugurated the new organ with two recitals on October 1 and 2, 1895. "A instrument quickened into life by the touch of the master hand," declared the *Star's* music critic. "The splendid instrument afforded Archer an opportunity to display the wonderful technique and brilliant powers of orchestration with which he is endowed. The various numbers of the program were as dissimilar as it was possible, yet Mr. Archer was perfectly at home in each of them. The instrument itself is mellow and rich in tone, and capable of great volume when the full organ is being utilised. The combinations evidently have been carefully selected and in their variety and excellence of their registrations and tonal qualities may legitimately be considered equal to those of any other organ in the city." Archer's program included Lemmen's "Sonata Pontificale," Saint-Saëns' "March Héroïque," Widor's "Toccata," and the overture from Wagner's *Tannhaüser*. The pope's personal chamberlain Msgr. Henry O'Bryan was in attendance, and it was expected he would preside over ceremonies in November to rededicate the newly decorated church. However, on October 20 he collapsed at the high altar while celebrating mass and four days later died of a heart attack. O'Bryan was no stranger to Montreal. A long-time friend of Father Dowd's, he had vacationed in Canada for seven summers and was a frequent guest at the presbytery. His funeral was held at Saint Patrick's on October 26, and because of his position of papal ablegate outranked even that of a cardinal, O'Bryan was buried in the cathedral. (An ablegate is responsible for delivering insignia from the Vatican to a newly appointed cardinal. As custodian of the cardinal's symbols of office, he is the middle man between the pope and his princes, and as such protocol ranks him ahead of a cardinal.)

Saint Patrick's officially reopened on Sunday, November 10, 1895 and according to the *Star,* "as far as the interior is concerned it is a new church … one of the prettiest and most complete ecclesiastical structures in the city." It had been simplified for monumental effect, and the visual result was massively calm and strong.

> The altar now presents a more symmetrical appearance than hitherto. The main altar and sanctuary have been fitted up with hundreds of incandescent lights which tremble and scintillate from every pinnacle, producing a brilliant and inspiring effect. The decorations of the sanctuary are superb. It is here that the acme of perfection is reached. The vault of the apse is one mass of gold, yellow and green. Gold mosaic forms a resplendent background upon which are traced in their natural colours large clusters of the foliage and blossom of the passion flower. The cornice and ribs of the groined ceiling in the apse are decorated in a pretty shade of green, while the capitals at the top of the dark

Sienna marble columns are faithful imitations of Grecian bronze. Over the high altar and upon the wall are the papal arms, while immediately underneath and filling the space between the arches and the cornices are magnificent frescos representative of the adoring angels.

The *True Witness and Catholic Chronicle* was equally effusive.

The result is infallibly ... so delicate, so lightsome, so harmonic, so soothing, so refining, that a stranger on entering draws irresistibly back, as if struck by some glorious apparition, and the sense of peace, combined with an elevation that steals over the observer, seems to mysteriously force the dazzled mind to pause—and to adore.

The massive brass sanctuary lamp was designed by Locke. It is 22 feet high and weighs a ton. Attached to the framework are six angels, crowned by a halo of crosses and fleur-de-lys. They bear shields with various steno-graphic symbols: the Alpha and Omega, used to designate God the Father; the IHS acrostic for Jesus Christ, Son of God and Saviour; a PX Christogram, and a Latin and Greek Cross. Below the angels hangs a Celtic cross. Between the pedestals in the base are coloured glass ornaments that are seen to their best advantage when the lamp is lit. During the renovations, Plamondon's paintings of the Stations of the Cross* were regrettably replaced with a series painted in 1847 by an Italian artist, Anthony Petriglia.

In 1897 Saint Patrick's observed its diamond jubilee, and by then the controlling Irish faction had shouldered its way into the resistant ranks of the urban Protestant establishment. Renting a pew in Saint Patrick's was a social statement that put its holder on the A-list of leading English-speaking Catholics in Montreal. Significantly, the fraternity of influential Catholics in the parish founded the first Council of the Knights of Columbus in Canada

---

*Eight of the 14 had to be destroyed in the early 1920s because they weren't properly stored; the remaining six were sold to the Institute des Sourds Muets in 1933, and acquired by the Montreal Museum of Fine Arts in 1961.

the same year. James John Guérin, a member of the congregation who was later elected mayor of Montreal, went on to become Canada's first Grand Knight.

A mass composed by Professor J. A. Fowler was commissioned for the jubilee and the *Herald*'s critic deemed it "a grand success. It is bright and melodious and the harmony is rich and as large as is needed for such an occasion. The choir, assisted by a good orchestra and accompanied by the beautiful organ, rendered the mass in most perfect manner. The solos were also well rendered." During the mass a gift from Pope Leo XIII was added to the church—a life size wax effigy* of St. Patrick, as well as a piece of bone believed to be a relic of the saint. The figure was dressed in "a cassock of purple silk, the alb of white lace, and the chasuble, stole and maniple of green silk trimmed with alternate bands of purple velvet and gold braid. All of these vestments are identical to in shape and colour to those at present used by the bishops of the Roman Catholic Church. The single exception is the chausable which is of the ancient Gothic pattern, a style at present worn by priests of the Roman Catholic Church in England when officiating at the mass. A miter of gold cloth heavily embroidered and jewelled, surmounts the head of the figure, and crosier of silver gilt reposes in the left hand. The feet are shod with a pair of leather sandals. On the third finger of the right hand is the episcopal ring of gold set with a large amethyst."

The effigy was installed in the frontal one of four new side altars that were added. St. Patrick's altar in the southeast corner of the church was donated by Patrick Mullin, of whom nothing is known, and initially dedicated to the Holy Angels in memory of his wife and son. St. Ann's altar in the northwest corner of the church is a memorial to federal Senator Edward Murphy, a hardware tycoon who collapsed and died on the sidewalk in front of Saint Patrick's on December 5, 1895. St. Anthony's altar in the south west corner is a memorial to Quebec Senator James O'Brien and his wife. O'Brien had come from Aughnagar, County Tyrone, and opened a dry goods business in Montreal. He died in 1903. The carved bas-relief on the altar frontal shows naked bodies writhing in the flames of purgatory.

*The wax image of Saint Patrick deteriorated and was burned in 1993, and the ashes buried in the church. In 1996, when the baptismal font was installed on the right side of the high altar in front of the original St. Joseph's altar the Holy Angels' altar was rededicated in honour of St. Joseph.

Angels quench the thirst of the souls as they reach through the flames to touch the Virgin Mary enshrined on a cloud. It is meant to be an allegory, but it has frightened generations of youngsters who got a perfect child's-eye-level glimpse of the seething cauldron of torture. The Sacred Heart altar in the north-east corner is a gift from the first head-warden of Saint Patrick's, Michael Burke, who was vice president of the City & District Savings Bank, and from his sister Elizabeth Anne. The new altars were consecrated on Sunday, June 18, 1899, by the Right Rev. Alexander Macdonnell, bishop of Alexandria.

The same year work was begun on the pictorial Litany of the Saints in the 200 open panels of the wainscotting. Work on the series continues to this day. (See Appendix Two for list of saints).

The final touch was the installation of the stone image of St. Patrick outside on a perch 60 feet above the main doors. The statue, exposed to the sun , and snow and rain, has its hand raised in constant blessing, no matter what grief or joy those in the city below might cause. With the church completely remodeled, Quinlivan turned his attention to building an English-language high school. In those days Irish Catholics had no secondary schools of their own, so they went to French schools where they were taught in English. Quinlivan set out to rectify the situation, and laid the cornerstone for the high school on September 18, 1898. It opened the following year.* The school was bilingual, open to both English- and French-speaking Catholics.

"The mission of the school is for untold good. Within its walls will mingle the intellectual sons of the two great races, and that *bonne entente* of which we read in the newspapers will then become a reality," Quinlivan wrote. "The young men there will learn to speak each other's language and understand each other's mentality, and just so far as this is accomplished, will old differences lessen and finally disappear."

Quinlivan was also instrumental in erecting a monument at Cap des Rosiers on the Gaspé Peninsula to the 180 Irish who drowned on May 23, 1847 when the immigrant ship *Carrick* encountered an unseasonable blizzard and broke up on rocks off the Gaspé coast. "Father Quinlivan's name is cut

---

*The school stood on property that had once belonged to Mayor Mills at what is today the intersection of University Street and de la Gauchetière. It was sold in 1916,and became Belmont School. It was torn down in 1947 to make way for the extension of University.

in the granite, but it is not less permanently imprinted upon the breasts of a grateful people," one Irish resident from the Gaspé remarked after the unveiling.

Queen Victoria died in January 1901. Although she was universally revered, her Britannic majesty did not figure heavily in the affections of her Canadian subjects of Irish ancestry. Daniel Gallery, Liberal MP and city councillor, perhaps best summed up the prevailing attitude: "As an Irishman I should express the sentiments of the vast majority of the people of my race when I state how much more esteemed was Queen Victoria to the Irish than many of her predecessors." Bishop Bruchési issued a pastoral letter which acknowledged that while "Catholics of the diocese join in universal sorrow on the occasion of the death of the Queen," it was at the same time prohibited "to display all emblems of mourning for the head of a Creed other than ours." So the prayers offered at Saint Patrick's during the Empire's day of official mourning on January 27 were not for the Queen per se, but "for the woman, faithful during 60 years to her duties of queen, of wife, of mother, whose qualities and virtues cause sovereigns to be loved by God and man." Quinlivan seemed surprised that anyone would expect a mass to be said for Victoria especially since she once declared that "the sacrifice of the mass now used by the Church of Rome is superstitious and idolatrous. However great our love for her memory," Quinlivan observed, "it would be hypocritical for us to perform a sacred rite which she so unsparingly condemned." A slightly contradictory message about world leaders was preached eight months later, however, when American President William McKinley was assassinated in September. "The church commands us to pray for the preservation of all rulers, spiritual and temporal," Father Callaghan said in a sermon after the shooting. "In the present instance, we are called upon to sympathize not with a distant nation, but with a kindred and neighbourly people. When Americans weep, Canadians shed tears over their great calamities." Notice was also taken of the fact that McKinley was of Irish stock. The fact that he was Protestant made no difference— McKinley was a third generation American, but his roots were Irish.

Shortly afterwards Father Quinlivan's personality changed. He complained of migraines and of a chronic sinus condition and became contrary and uncharacteristically short-tempered and belligerent. When Mayor McShane's niece came calling, her uncle was startled to learn that she "received a harsh reception from Father Quinlivan. So much was this marked that she wished the floor would open and swallow her. After hearing her name and other information, he grew quite pleasant."

In truth, Quinlivan was dying. In the summer of 1901 he took a six-month leave of absence to visit his father in Minnesota. While there, the pastor of St. Wendeline's church in Luxemberg gave him a 12th-century crucifix that originally came from a Cicerstian Abbey on the Baltic. It is one of Saint Patrick's treasures and today hangs in the sacristy. On his way back to Montreal, Quinlivan sought treatment for his mysterious illness in Boston and was operated upon in New York. His health continued to fail. on the first Sunday in Lent, February 16, 1902, Father Quinlivan wandered through Saint Patrick's as if seeing the church for the last time. At each of the seven altars he knelt and prayed. The following morning he left for Paris to consult French medical specialists. There he died on March 12. "The melancholy tidings were conveyed in a cablegram," the *Herald* reported, and the news soon spread, for the dead priest was popular and well known in all sections of Montreal, and it came as a shock to his parisioners. "The door bell and the telephone in the presbytery are constantly ringing. People all over the city are calling to express regret. They recall the considerate bearing of Father Quinlivan towards those of his congregation. He was never too busy nor too tired to hear the tale of those in trouble, and all felt that he was their friend as well as their spiritual advisor." He was buried in France in Montparnasse cemetery. "His noblest monument will be Saint Patrick's church," the *Gazette* eulogised, "the interior decoration of which he carried out in a manner that showed his artistic skill and his deep veneration for the House of God."

Chapter Eight

A GENTLE MORALIST and good-humoured evangelist with a knack for making converts, Martin Callaghan was the first priest from Montreal to become pastor of Saint Patrick's. Callaghan was born in Griffintown on November 20, 1846, and was one of three brothers who entered the priesthood. To distinguish them they went not by their family name but by their first names: Father Martin, Father Luke, and Father James. Martin joined the Sulpicians in 1869 and was ordained on December 21, 1872. He was a natural social worker. Having been raised in a slum neighbourhood he identified with the poor and the dispossessed. Children took to him instantly, and Callaghan sought to establish an active ministry among marginal groups. He opened one of the first social centres for Montreal's emerging Black community in 1870. But it was among the Chinese that he made his mark. Hearing of a Chinese immigrant who wanted to be baptised, Callaghan instructed not only the immigrant but the immigrant's son and cousin. All three were baptised, and all three became proselytizers for the faith. They brought so many converts that a Chinese Catholic parish was established in Montreal. Another story tells of a young Danish woman who arrived at the presbytery looking for a place to stay. Callaghan found accommodation for her, and she, too, decided to come into the Catholic communion. She eventually returned to Denmark where she became a nun. Later she went to Iceland and founded a convent. "No cleric here or elsewhere had so extensive a coterie of non-Catholic acquaintances," said a friend. "The number of conversions accredited to him runs into the thousands. Indeed, his fame in this special ministry entitled him to the name of arch-convert maker, and made him sought after by other priests anxious to learn the secrets of his remarkable success." It may have been because he preached what he described as the notion of "continuous conversions" which taught that people can, in spite of their failings, renew their faith again and again. His first major assignment as pastor was to preside over the civic funeral for

Alderman Frank Hart, who died in Colorado Springs, Colorado in March. According to the *Herald*, "Saint Patrick's church, on pillar, wall, and arch was draped in black and purple and gold, for the funeral" and the church was jammed with municipal officials, including the mayor and every city councillor.

Because Callaghan was the first pastor to be appointed by the diocese instead of by the Sulpicians, he never managed to shake the impression that he was Bishop Bruchési's sycophant. The bishop had to assure the congregation personally that there was nothing underhanded in the change, and that Callaghan's autonomy in dealing with his communicants would be respected. Bruchési had himself risen through the ranks of the Sulpicians and pledged

> not do anything to destroy a nationality. On the contrary, I will do all that is in my power to sympathise with all nationalities and strengthen them, because I know that if we French Canadians are proud of our language, and attached to our dear traditions, the English and the Irish are also proud of their languages, and are also attached to the traditions of their ancestors.
>
> Let the Irish be Irish, let the English be English, and let the French Canadians be French Canadian. But we must never forget that both languages—French and English— are official in our province and in our city. We must live together as brethren and as members of the same family.

It was during Callaghan's term as pastor that the parish's indebtedness to the Seminary of St. Sulpice was at last paid in full. For the first time in 55 years the Saint Patrick's fabrique had clear title to its own church. Saint Patrick's first board of wardens* was elected on March 29, 1903, and on May 3 they burned the mortgage. On May 13,the Sulpicians surrendered the title to the church. According to ecclesiastical law, a church cannot be consecrated until it is paid for in full. On Tuesday June 26, 1906 Archbishop

---

*Michael Burke, Martin Eagan, Peter McCaffrey, Felix Casey, Timothy Crowe, John Hammill, A.D. McGillis, Charles Smith, James Rogers, Patrick Reynolds, Patrick McCrory, and Dr. J. A. Macdonald.

Paul Bruchési consecrated the church in an ancient ceremony that recalls Moses anointing the Arc of the Covenant. The altars were stripped and the outline of a large cross sprinkled with salt and ashes was drawn in the centre of the nave. According to custom, only the clergy are present for the consecration and three bishops and eight priests from across Canada assisted Msgr. Bruchési. The plainchant of Solesmes was sung for the first time in Montreal during the five-hour service. When it was over, the doors were opened to the public. "The church was superbly ornamented for the celebration, a white canopy adorning the entrance, while a handsome raised dais with a throne had been prepared for Msgr. Bruchesi in the sanctuary, and from a centre trophy long draperies of yellow, blue and crimson streamed to the corners of the edifice," reported the *Gazette*. "All these, combined with the gorgeous vestments of the clergy and the acolytes, contrasting with the sombre masses of the congregation which crowded the church by day and night and formed an ensemble of marvellous beauty." To commemorate the occasion, twelve mural crosses (representing the twelve apostles) engraved in marble, each with its own candle bracket, were anointed and installed in the walls of the nave. In the absence of documentation, the crosses prove that the church has been consecrated. In his sermon, Bishop Bruchési described the occasion as the greatest event in the history of the parish and, adding a personal note, recalled that he had been born and grew up almost within the shadow of its walls. As a child, he said, he had often stopped into Saint Patrick's to pray. "I am neither the pastor of the French nor of the English, nor of the Irish. I am the bishop of the diocese," he said. "While I regard all as my spiritual children, I must acknowledge those who have done much, and I must say I am proud of the Irish Catholics and of the noble work they have done." Then raising his hand in benediction, he spoke the words many in the congregation had waited a lifetime to hear: "Your church is at last free from debt, your generosity is well known. Do not forget those who laboured for you and who today rest from their labours."

At a reception that evening at the Windsor Hotel Father Callaghan spoke briefly to the 150 guests. Callaghan, who had been born four months before the church opened, said simply, "I thank God for the gift of having seen with my own eyes the dawn of this day. It is a day which reminds us of all those hailing from the north, south, east, and west of Ireland who sought a home on the island of Montreal in the beautiful city of Mary, as well as all of those who boast of being their descendants—a day which recalls what they proved to be and what they accomplished—a day which brings to memory all that happened to them and all that concerned them during an interval of a century. Saint Patrick's is a parish that may yet be equalled, but never surpassed." Then, as the invited guests left the hotel after the banquet, a cipher of electric lights that spelled SP (Saint Patrick's) on the west wall of the church, and an electric cross atop the spire were switched on and illuminated the night sky.

One of the simplest funerals at the church for a celebrated public figure took place at Saint Patrick's on February 21, 1907 when Sir William Hales Hingston was buried. The former mayor had been knighted by Queen Victoria in 1895 and had been appointed to the Senate. The interior of the church was draped in black and gold for the occasion, but as the *Star* reported, the funeral broke with convention because it "was of the simplest character possible. There were no flowers and the body lay in a black cloth casket with a plate upon it containing the words, William Hales Hingston." Although the church was filled to overflowing with dignitaries, and old-timers said it was the biggest funeral in the church since D'Arcy McGee's, the obsequies were, at Dr. Hingston's request, minimal. "It always shocked him that death should be made an occasion for display. He loved flowers but believed they had no place beside a corpse," Hingston's son, a Jesuit priest, told reporters.

Father Callaghan, one of three concelebrants at Hingston's funeral, was considered an interim pastor. He lacked the social graces and sophistication many of his well-heeled parishioners expected and he was never totally at ease in the wood-panelled drawing rooms of the Square Mile. He retired on the feast of the Immaculate Conception, December 8, 1907, to make way for his successor, and his departure was so sudden it was, the *Gazette* reported, "the occasion of no little agitation amongst certain portions of the congregation." While few in the parish knew of the coming change, the *Gazette* announced on a Saturday morning that Callaghan had resigned after 35 years connection with the church. Many were shocked he was leaving.

"My every wish has been for the good of Saint Patrick's," he said, "and now my active working days are over. Being faithful to the sacred trust confided in me by my venerable predecessors, Fathers Dowd and Quinlivan,

I will pass over the affairs of the church not to a more devoted or able, but to a younger man." A *Gazette* editorial suggested Callaghan "had grown old in the service of Saint Patrick's."

" He has been a faithful priest, a sure adviser, and while a good Irishman, his voice has always been raised in the cause of peace and good will."

Callaghan was only 51 years old when he retired. He died of pneumonia at the Hôtel Dieu Hospital on June 10, 1915. His brother Luke, also a priest, celebrated the requiem funeral mass at Notre Dame, and at his own request, Martin Callaghan was buried, "in a plain wooden coffin, without elaborate finishings, ornaments or flowers," in the crypt of the Sulpician Seminary on Sherbrooke Street.

Martin Callaghan was a natural social worker. Raised in Griffintown, he identified with the poor and the dispossessed.
Photo by William Notman & Son. Courtesy of Saint Patrick's Basilica.

Chapter Nine

"I HOPE TO GET RID of my child-like appearance before I reach Montreal, otherwise I'll have no authority," Father Gerald McShane wrote to his sister Alice from Paris shortly after he was ordained there in September 1897. He was 24 but looked like a teenager. "I have not done much parish work beyond a few sick calls, a funeral and giving a few people the (temperance) pledge," he wrote. "I have to roar laughing at the funny remarks made about my youthfulness. Some will not believe I am ordained until they see me saying mass."

A scant ten years later McShane became pastor of Saint Patrick's. He was young for the job, but it was assumed he would do great things. He was brilliant, complex, strong willed, and well connected. One of his mentors and an important benefactor was Lord Thomas Shaugnessey, the president of the Canadian Pacific Railway. Another was James Guérin, a member of the church who was elected mayor of Montreal shortly after McShane became pastor. For the next 48 years no one ever again doubted McShane's ability or ever questioned his authority. "He grew old fast. I only remember him as a formidable man with white hair," recalled Emmett Cardinal Carter, who, as a ten-year-old in 1922 served 7 a.m. mass for McShane every morning at Saint Patrick's. "He was a very efficient pastor," Carter remembers, "but very hard."

Gerald Joseph McShane was born into a patrician Irish Montreal family on December 5, 1872, and was baptised at Saint Patrick's. His parents died when he was still a child and he was raised in an orderly, business-like atmosphere of religion, politics and public service by his uncle, James McShane, a prominent politician and former mayor and the city's harbour master. McShane's route to Holy Orders was typical. He went to Belmont School, and studied classics at the Collège de Montréal where he was described as "a regular and studious pupil." When he graduated he came third in his class of 24. In 1896 he joined the Gentlemen of St. Sulpice in

Paris. He was ordained by Cardinal Richard. He described the service in one of his many letters to his sister. "Our retreat was made at Issy. There in silence and in peace among the flowers and in the pretty gardens, the nearest place to heaven, I prepared with my companions for the greatest day in my life," he wrote.

The ceremony began at 7:30 p.m. and lasted only two hours and a half. The good venerable old cardinal went through everything in a manner that would edify and impress any onlooker. There were in all 12 taking part. I felt exceptionally blessed at being ordained by the saintly cardinal and among students and priests, three-quarters whom were well known to me.

The first Mass I said was in honour of the first saint of America, Rose of Lima; the second was for the repose of mother's and father's souls. What I have not told you, and what I shall never be able to tell you, is the change that has taken place in me since I've been promoted to the unspeakable dignity of the priesthood. Oh, that I might describe to you the sweetness of the consolations that are poured into the soul of a newly ordained priest as he ascends for the first time the altar steps to hold our Divine Lord in his hands, to minister Him to others after having created Him by a few words from his lips!

I always had a very high expectation of a priest's happiness and exalted privilege, yes, but my idea was but a very dim and imperfect shade of what the reality proved to be.

Do not forget to pray for me, that I may be a good priest. A priest's dignity is great, but his responsibilities are awful to think of, for to him he has the care of not only saving his own soul but of saving the souls of hundreds of others.

McShane ministered in Ireland and in Italy before returning to Montreal in 1903. Initially he was assigned to Notre Dame and made his reputation at the parish church preaching in French. He also became the first Roman Catholic chaplain at McGill University, where in 1904 he started the Columbian Club, which later became the Newman Club. His early correspondence reveals that he was not as dour or as serious a person as he appeared to be later in life. "I have fallen victim to the bicycle mania," he confessed in one of his letters. "Last Monday afternoon I received a few tips on riding. I mounted the machine with a little difficulty but that very night I rented a wheel for a fortnight and the next day rode a half a mile on it. Then on the morrow I rode successfully about six miles without any more fatal mishaps than the loss of a leg ... from a pair of trousers which was carried off by the pedals through my neglecting to procure clasps for my feet. Oh, life is not worth living without a bike!!! That is the conclusion I've come to after many interesting tours in the vicinity."

McShane's first task upon being named pastor of Saint Patrick's was to help organise the first International Eucharistic Congress ever to be held in North America. More than 200,000 people, including foreign cardinals, bishops and priests, were expected in September 1910 for what might be described as a religious Expo. Saint Patrick's was assigned responsibility for the English-speaking delegates.

One Sunday morning in 1908, *Charlotte*, the old bell the Sulpicians gave to Saint Patrick's, cracked while being tolled and, as one reporter put it, "a harsh jangle succeeded its sweet peal." The accident proved to be fortuitous; it enabled McShane to have a carillon commissioned and installed in time for the convention. (See Appendix Four for the bells and their inscriptions). *Charlotte* came down from the bell tower in July 1908 and was sent to London to be recast. It was rehung with eight new bells on May 14, 1910, a week after King Edward VII died. Edward VII was probably the last monarch to be regarded with genuine affection in Quebec, and ironically, one of the bells is dedicated to the king, not because McShane especially wanted it so, but because the bell's corporate sponsor, the CPR, insisted upon it. The ecumenical gesture was applauded in a letter to the *Herald*. "It speaks well for the broad-mindedness of the Roman Catholics of Canada that the name of the head of the Church of England is engraved on the bell. This is the only instance since the Reformation of an English sovereign being thus honoured in perpetuity by the Roman Catholic church in its religious observances."

The additional bells were named in honour of our Lady of the Most Blessed Sacrament, the pope, the papal legate, the archbishop, Fathers Dowd, Quinlivan, and McShane, and a teaching nun, Rev. Mother Sister St. Aloysis, superior of St. Patrick's Academy. Sister St. Aloysis was born Marie Sarah Donnelly in 1844, became a nun in 1864 and joined St. Patrick's Academy in 1876. She died in 1925.

The bells chimed for the first time that September to signal the beginning of the third International Eucharistic Congress, a convention described by the *Montreal Star* as "the most remarkable gathering of Roman Catholics ever to take place on American soil."

The Congress was inaugurated on September 5 by Vincenze Vannutelli, the papal legate. During the week-long convention Saint Patrick's was home to Cardinal Logue, Archbishop of Armagh and Primate of Ireland. The British Jesuit Bernard Vaughan delivered the sermon at the opening session. He talked about changing mores and his words continue to resonate almost a century later. "We are living in a day of headlines, snapshots, telephones, taxicabs and music halls. It is a day of fever, fret and fume, when competition is so keen and the margin of profit so fine … a day when high ideals are yielding to the pressure of creature comforts, when self-sacrificing Catholicism is being bartered for self-centred materialism, and the Christian sense of sin is a bygone superstition; in a day when it matters not what you believe, but only what you do and when you may do what you like provided when you are not found out." The only unsettling incident during the congress was the sermon delivered at Notre Dame by Archbishop Bourne of Westminster in which he suggested that the English language was the only way of bringing the Catholic faith to Canada. "It would be a matter of extreme regret were the French language, so long the one exponent of religion, culture, and progress in this land, ever to lose any portion of the consideration and cultivation which it now enjoys," said Bourne. That statement is overlooked by French Canadian historians, who seize on what he said next: "But no one can close his eyes to the fact that if Canada is to be won and held for the Catholic Church, this can only be done through the medium of our English speech. In other words, the future of the church in Canada will depend to an enormous degree upon the extent to which the power, influence, and prestige of the English language and literature can be

"I hope to get rid of my child-like appearance before I reach Montreal, otherwise I'll have no authority," Father Gerald McShane wrote to his sister in 1897. Ten years later he became pastor of Saint Patrick's. *Photo by Gordon. Courtesy of Saint Patrick's Basilica.*

Pastor McShane, seated (left), and Sir Wilfrid Laurier, standing (top rt),
in the presence of Cardinal Logue (centre) at the first
International Eucharistic Congress ever to be held in North
America. It took place in Montreal in 1910. More than 200,000 people,
including foreign cardinals, bishops, and priests attended.
Courtesy of Saint Patrick's Basilica.

definitely placed upon the side of the Catholic Church." Bourne was rebuked for his lack of diplomacy by Quebec nationalist Henri Bourassa, who replied that while "French Canadians are but a handful, Christ did not require them to deny their language as a condition of faith. Do not take away from men their language, that which is dearest to them after their Faith in God."

Saint Patrick's was filled to capacity for special services all week. On Friday there was a concert of choral music by the St. Paul's Cathedral choir from Pittsburgh. "Finer singing has been heard here," wrote one critic, "but we seldom have an opportunity of enjoying so comprehensive a range of selections given with such studious sincerity." On Saturday Cardinal Logue celebrated a pontifical mass at Saint Patrick's which was described as the most impressive at the congress,

> from the standpoint of the solemnity of service, the elaborate preparation, the beauty of the musical program and the hundreds of worshippers who crowded through the portals of the church or thronged the grounds to witness the procession into the church.
>
> Surely, old Saint Patrick's never looked grander, never more imposing. The fence surrounding the large grounds of the church was fairly smothered in a billowing sea of bunting, flags and banners and streamers fluttered and snapped in the breeze. The interior of the church was all that good taste and artistic conception could create. In addition to the wealth of colour in the sanctuary and the body of the church, the climbing vines winding round the pillars added a touch of beauty which no bunting could ever have given.

During the service the papal legate dropped in unexpectedly to bless the Irish of Montreal. The congress ended Sunday with another pontifical mass at Saint Patrick's celebrated by Canada's youngest bishop, Michael Fallon, from London, Ont. That was followed by a four-hour Eucharistic procession from Notre Dame to a shrine in Fletcher's Field in a parade which the *New York Times* described as "the most remarkable religious demonstration ever witnessed in North America ... numbering at a modest estimate, half a million." As a permanent memorial of the Eucharistic Congress, Congress Gate was built below the church on La Gauchetière near St. Alexandre. For his part in making the congress a success the Saint Patrick's choir expressed its appreciation by giving McShane "a pair of gold-mounted opera glasses and a handsome portable reading lamp of hammered brass."

In 1911, McShane instigated changes to the Saint Patrick's Day parade that weren't universally applauded. He decided to hold the parade before the 11 a.m. mass instead of after. It began at 9:00 a.m. instead of at noon. McShane took his place in the carriage with Mayor Guérin, and two of Montreal's most celebrated Irish grandees waved to the crowds. The 9 a.m starting time was short-lived. After 1912 it reverted to the afternoon.

In April 1912 one of Saint Patrick's more popular young parishioners, 25-year-old Quigg Baxter drowned in the sinking of the *Titanic*. Baxter was aboard the ship returning from Europe with his widowed mother and sister. His father had been a prominent diamond merchant who had built the Baxter Block on St. Lawrence Boulevard; his mother claimed Quebec heroine Madeleine de Verchères as an ancestor. He had been baptised in Saint Patrick's, had been an altar boy at the church, and, until he lost his eye in a game, had been a star player with the Shamrocks hockey team. His body was never recovered, and a memorial service for him and the *Titanic*'s victims was held in the church on April 21, 1912. During the memorial mass, the *Gazette* reported that

Father McShane made delicate and touching allusion to the lamented president of the Grand Trunk Railway, recalling Mr. Charles M. Hays' [another Montrealer who drowned in the wreck] kindly courtesy and respect to Cardinal Logue when his eminence visited Saint Patrick's two years ago. On that occasion Cardinal Logue enjoyed on board the private car of President Hays every mark of respect and affection and the people of Saint Patrick's would not soon forget the kindness of the President at that time.

At the conclusion of the high mass the black pall used at solemn funeral services was spread over the sanctuary railing, along which the sanctuary boys in black cassocks

and white surplices were ranged, headed by the acolytes
and subdeacon bearing the cross … Father McShane chanted
the prayers for the dead … and spoke feelingly of the event.

"'The sorrowful circumstances of the appalling disaster," he said, "the
number and the prominence of the victims, the heroism and Christian
fortitude displayed upon that memorable night have aroused in our hearts
feelings of prayerful sympathy and compassion. We are members of a church
that, like her Divine founder, is filled with tender pity and solicitude for
those who are in sorrow and weighed down under the burden of trial and
affliction. Let us ask the gentle Saviour to visit those desolate homes and
grief-stricken families with the refreshing aid of his comfort and consolation
and the spirit of true Christian resignation.'"

In 1913 McShane committed the parish to building a church hall in
time for the Canadian Eucharistic Congress to be held in Montreal in July
1915. Wardens authorised a $100,000 loan for the project and Toronto
architect James Patrick Hynes was engaged. The cornerstone was laid on
October 19, 1914. The building, one of the first in Montreal to be built of
concrete, was meant as a memorial to the 1910 Eucharistic Congress. On
the ground floor, with direct access to the church there would be the Lady
Chapel and a 700-seat auditorium, a rehearsal hall, board room, a baptistery,
a new sacristy and offices for the sacristan. The other two floors would
contain conference rooms and office space. Hynes described the style of
the building as "cubist," but not in the conventional sense. "The building
symbolises the mechanical age, which allows machines to make straight
lines, to have them plumb, level and parallel, thereby producing the square,
which when given the third dimension, produces the cube," he explained.
"The cube symbolism will be used in the altar in the Lady Chapel, in the
Celtic cross on the exterior decoration, and also in the crosses decorating
the pews and sacristy furniture."

At the same time, McShane was adamant that all the stained glass
windows in the church should be in place for the Canadian congress. It had
become too expensive to import windows from Austria so Alexander Locke,
who had designed the four small windows in the sanctuary, was contracted
to complete the work with windows that would complement the four
existing Tyrol Glasmerai windows. Locke submitted sketches of what he

had in mind. "I can see no reason why we should not have the windows in place by Christmas," he wrote McShane in the summer of 1912. "I assure you they will go along fast enough when we get working on them." He quoted a price of $1,360 for a big window;$750 for a small one. McShane, however, thought that was too expensive and wanted credit. Locke, understandably, preferred to be paid before he shipped the windows. McShane found himself "distressed and disappointed" by Locke's attitude. "I may tell you candidly that what determined me to place the order with you was the impression you made upon me at our first meeting a few years ago," McShane wrote to him. "Father Quinlivan frequently mentioned your name at the dinner table and entertained a high regard for your personality. I gathered from the deceased priest's remarks that our Saint Patrick's church of Montreal was one of the works to which you had undertaken to devote your very best ability; so that unlimited confidence in you was uppermost in my mind when I definitely decided to place the order with you. Now that I have committed myself with my people, in the pulpit and individually, to have the work done in a reasonable time, I find myself hopelessly placed without any definite agreement or promise from you. I leave for Europe in June, and my heaviest cross and greatest worry is that there is no mutual arrangement between us with regard to these windows. An exchange of letters will only delay and complicate matters. I am going to ask you for the sake of your old-time regard for our dear church and its late pastor to come up and spend a day in Montreal. We will have a heart-to-heart talk over the matter, and I can assure you that, regarding the time limit for this work, I will be reasonable and amenable." Perhaps McShane was being fiscally prudent, or perhaps he felt that because Locke was the nephew of the apostolic delegate to Canada, Saint Patrick's was entitled to preferential treatment. It wasn't that Locke didn't want the work. As he made clear in his letters, he simply couldn't meet the deadlines set by McShane.

"It isn't my going to Montreal that troubles me," Locke replied in one of his many letters, "but when I know the work I have to tackle, I am at a loss to know what to say regarding the windows. I cannot see my way clear to doing them this year," he wrote.

> I have underway at least between 30 and 40 figure windows,
> not counting the contract for the Bishop of New York that

is still unfinished. It isn't going to Montreal that bothers me, so much as when I could finish your windows. I am endeavouring to get more help in this line and find it almost impossible to secure the right kind of men. You may be sure that it goes very much against me to have to write to you in this strain, for believe me, I have a very soft spot in my heart for Saint Patrick's.

Much of their correspondence is missing, but from the tone of the letters that are on file, McShane refused to take no for an answer and bullied Locke into doing the work. By the autumn of 1913, Locke at last promised McShane "perfect windows in every respect, windows that will be worthy of the church they are going in." For the next two years McShane seems to have been obsessed with the windows. He thrived on minutiae and endlessly second-guessed the artist over apparently picayune matters. "Regarding St. Columba, permit me to suggest that you make a drastic change in the treatment of the window," McShane suggested to Locke in one letter. "I have made a special study of this saint's life and I would prefer you make the following changes:

> I would like this saint represented as an abbot about 60 years old—bearded, tall, handsome and graceful, wearing pontifical insignia, but not so ornate as those of a bishop. These insignia should include mitre, pectoral cross, ring, crozier or pastoral staff. I would suggest he carry in one hand the book of the Gospels, as he was essentially a missionary. Moreover, you could place a kingly crown under his foot as he denounced succession to the throne. He was of the clan O'Donnell, and if you would like to use their coat of arms, I send it to you herewith. Now as to the scene: I would prefer you represent Columba as a monk, without pontifical insignia, embarked on a boat which is slowly moving out from the Irish shore. The boat, which, of course is of a primitive make, is manned by Columba's companions, monks. History says there were 12 of them. One of the monks, young, handsome is at the bow and holds a large cross in hand, turning towards the sea.

Columba, sad and tearful, waves farewell to the Irish shore or blesses the assembled people on the water's edge. On the shore are his kinsfolk. On the shore could also be depicted a monastery and church near an oak grove—these buildings to represent the large number of schools, monasteries and churches which he had founded in Ireland. I trust I am not imposing too much of a task in asking you to treat St. Columba's window in this manner.

Similarly, in another letter McShane was critical of Locke's stained glass portrait of St. Margaret of Scotland. "I do not like the face, hair, or neck." He was blunt. "I think you can improve upon the head and make it more matron-like." Locke, of course, made the changes, but charged extra for the additional work. He submitted a bill for $1,500 for a big window and $950 for a small one. "I am surprised at the figures," McShane replied, "however, if the work is to be done as promptly as promised, and if I am not to put to extra expense, I shall be satisfied." The church was not as financially strapped as McShane led Locke to believe. The fact is, church revenues had never been better. Between 1913 and 1917 they more than doubled from $54,000 a year to $120,000.

Even as McShane haggled with Locke over the price of the windows, wardens approved a $25,000 loan to help the Shamrocks build a clubhouse even though the hockey team had no collateral and no prospect of securing a loan elsewhere. The team's request for the money out of church revenues was irregular, but McShane persuaded the wardens to approve the advance. "While the church is held to be cautious in the administration of its trust, we are also entrusted with the spiritual and moral welfare, and in this respect are empowered to spend the money," he said. That was consistent with McShane's belief that "the basis of all successful mentality is a good physique." Gladstone put it differently: "to succeed a man must be a good animal."

World War I broke out in August 1914, and many "good, human animals" would be slaughtered in what Henry James called the "abyss of blood and darkness." The war coincided with growing political tension in Ireland, which made it difficult for the congregation at Saint Patrick's to support England in the war.

Initially support for the war effort at Saint Patrick's was passive. A passion play was staged on Sunday, October 11, 1914 to raise money for the Canadian Patriotic Fund, a charity which had been set up to "assist families in distress as a result of breadwinners being thrown out of work through the war." It was the first time the church was used as a theatre, and the play, performed by volunteers, proved to be so successful it was repeated annually for years afterwards. In his sermons, McShane didn't talk about the war, but had to break his silence in June 1915 after a German U-boat attacked and sank the luxury liner *Lusitania* off the coast of Ireland. "It can hardly be expected that the Irishman will fly to the rescue of Britain in danger with the same spontaneity and alacrity of spirit as those who have no past or present grievance against British rule," McShane told his congregation shortly after the sinking.

> If an Irish father and mother, after a certain amount of legitimate hesitancy, give their full consent to their Canadian son to don a uniform and fight for a flag, that has not in the past been able to win a full measure of their loyalty and allegiance … if, I say, such a father and such a mother give the consent only after an inward struggle and the stifling of old feelings and the assurance that bygones will be bygones, and that pledges will be redeemed, I say that our English fellow citizens will be the first to acknowledge that such an inward victory, such a revulsion of feeling, deserves a full measure of recognition. If we can judge by the deeds performed by the Irish in this war, such a recruit is worth perhaps more to English arms than the fighting of those who have no such obstacles to overcome, no such feelings to stifle their hearts.

McShane said that while he would not advise anyone to enlist, he would encourage men to defend "Canada and Ireland."

> I will say that Canada and the preservation of Canadian privileges has a positive claim upon the services of every fit and free young man. There is a call and a mission of character so sacred that no man in all good conscience can

stifle it in his heart and leave it undeeded. I regard a soldier's profession as a real vocation. I regard the entrance into that profession as a call as sacred and as God-inspired as the call to any particular career or avocation in life. There is no feeling of the human soul so pure and as sublime as love of country as there is no act of man so noble as that of dying for his country, as there is no profession so grand and so worthy of admiration as the mission of the soldier who fights for his country.

In the end, 188 of Saint Patrick's young men joined the 199th Battalion Irish Canadian Rangers and saw action during the war; 88 of them, including Lord Shaugnessy's son Fred, were killed. The names of those who died are inscribed on the wall of honour on either side of the O'Brien memorial altar. (See Appendix Three).

While the parish was putting its energy into the war effort, McShane concentrated on finishing the church and Congress Hall. Money had been raised for the windows in the Lady Chapel in the new addition, but not for all of the windows in the church itself. Congress Hall eventually cost twice as much to build as planned— $193,145.54 to be precise, and McShane once again asked Locke for credit for "an indefinite period," so all ten windows could be installed at once. "I cannot tell you how disastrously the European War has affected collections of our people," he pleaded. Locke refused. By the spring of 1915 only six of the new windows were in place when Congress Hall informally opened with the screening of a Charlie Chaplin movie on April 7. Archbishop Bruchési blessed the building three months later on a stifling hot Sunday, July 11, 1915.

"Congress Hall was dedicated with all the grandeur the Catholic church can make use of on festive occasions," reported the *Star*. "Nearly 300 people took part in the procession, acolytes, sanctuary boys, the chancel choir, the men's choir, the visiting prelates in their violet robes, escorted by priests and a guard of honour composed of prominent men of the city." Among them, Quebec's Lieutenant-Governor, Pierre Evariste LeBlanc. The focal point of the Lady Chapel, the Madonna of the Smile was added in the spring of 1916. The statue of white Carrara marble is a copy of the original in Lisieux, France, which Saint Theresa, "the little flower of Jesus," venerated.

McShane had seen the statue during his trip abroad in 1913 and had it copied for Saint Patrick's.

The war dragged on and on Palm Sunday, April 16, 1916, a military mass was held at Saint Patrick's. Soldiers of the Irish Rangers marched through Congress grounds and into the church to take the places especially reserved for them in the sanctuary. Their regimental colours were unfurled and remained in the church until war's end. On the following Sunday, Easter Sunday, open rebellion broke out in Dublin and McShane offered prayers for the success of the rebels. "While we remember all too well that our country is at war, when we pray for peace, let the faith that we have and the blood that is in us, add a special word for Ireland, where there is now war within a war." The presence of the Union Jack and the regimental colours in the church especially antagonised members of the Ancient Order of Hibernians who refused to set foot inside Saint Patrick's "so long as England's cruel red was allowed to desecrate the temple." Many parishioners were sympathetic to the Irish revolutionaries. The more militant quit Saint Patrick's in protest against the battle flags and went to worship at St. Ann's. One of the indirect results of the controversy was the launching of a city-wide tag day to raise money for the wives and families of men sent overseas. Another was the initial meeting on November 17, 1917 of a women's organization whose mandate was to "intellectually, patriotically and socially" support both causes. Started by Mayor Guérin's sister, Bellelle, the Montreal chapter of the Catholic Women's League was the first CWL group in Canada. It proved to be so dynamic, it led to the foundation three years later of the national organisation.

Afraid that the Saint Patrick's Day parade in 1918 would turn into a riot against conscription, authorities cancelled it. "War Dimmed Feast of Ireland's Saint," trumpeted one newspaper headline that year. Solemn high mass was celebrated as usual, but because it was Passion Sunday the sanctuary and altar were "devoid of decoration with the exception of two massive chandeliers beside the high altar and a multitude of green lights about the shrine of Saint Patrick where the relics were exposed." As the luck of the Irish would have it, the Fifth Canadian Montreal Regiment came back from the war the following day and marched from Viger Station down Craig Street (today St. Antoine) to Griffintown. Members of the St. Ann's Young Mens Society and the Ancient Order of Hiberians stepped in behind and followed the soldiers through the streets. The impromptu parade may not have been officially sanctioned, but a parade there was, and as a result Montreal boasts that it is the only city in North America to have held a St. Patrick's Day parade every year without interruption since 1824.

By September 1918 the war was almost over, but in Montreal imminent victory was overshadowed by an outbreak of Spanish influenza. During the first week of October, people died at the rate of ten a day; by mid-October, it was 50 a day. The Board of Health closed all public meeting places, schools, theatres, and libraries. Bishop Bruchési closed the churches. "The epidemic is not diminishing, and it is necessary to use every means to stamp it out," the bishop decreed. "Large gatherings which present real dangers must be avoided." At Saint Patrick's, mass continued to be celebrated three times each day in the empty church on behalf of an absent congregation. On Sunday, October 20, McShane took communion door-to door to the faithful. "It was a unique religious event in the city's history," remarked the *Gazette*.

There was nothing essentially spectacular, as in the case of the Eucharistic Congress or as on Fête-Dieu. The host was not borne in glittering monstrance, but the ciborium was used. A pilot car containing a bugler prepared the people for the approach of a big limousine from which were hung clusters of flowers. The approach of the Blessed Sacrament was heralded by the ringing of a bell at which signal people came to the portals, knelt down and received the blessing. Rev. Father McShane, wearing a vestment of gold, and accompanied by surpliced altar boys, blessed each group of worshippers. From the windows of the car there also hung inscriptions inciting the people to prayer: 'Spare O Lord, spare Thy people and be not angry with them forever.' Not only the householders who came to their doors showed devout attention, but large numbers of pedestrians halted in the street and made their adoration.

McShane made the rounds for three hours until it began to snow.

World War I ended in November, but because of the epidemic Saint Patrick's didn't reopen to the public until Wednesday, December 18, so

McShane could bury his uncle and guardian, James, the former mayor who had died at the age of 85.

In January 1919 the Irish nationalist movement, Sinn Fein, proclaimed Ireland a republic, but British reinforcements moved in to suppress the Parliament. To show their solidarity with their homeland in the St. Patrick's Day parade that year Irishmen marched in the cold March rain behind the green, white, and orange flag of the new republic, the first occasion on which this emblem has been carried in Montreal. In his sermon at the church a visiting priest from New York referred to Ireland as " a land of sorrow," and asked the congregation to pray "for a full measure of liberty and true democracy, which is the God-given right of every free people." One of the consequences of the troubles in Ireland was that the St. Patrick's Day parade was becoming increasingly politicised. More unsettling were McShane's efforts to tamper with tradition; he clashed with the Hibernians over his wish to hold the parade on the Sunday nearest March 17 instead of on the patronal day. As a result of the ongoing tension, the church withdrew in 1923 from active participation in the planning of the parade. Ultimately, responsibility for the parade passed to a secular group, the United Irish Societies.

Bishop Bruchési became mentally unstable in 1920 and for the next two decades until he died he was bishop in name only. The administration of the diocese was carried on by Georges Gauthier, archbishop co-adjutor. Gauthier allowed McShane free reign to run Saint Patrick's with little interference, and McShane reinforced the all-enveloping cocoon of institutions—schools, nursing home, and orphanage—and he was a formidable influence within Montreal's English-speaking Catholic community. People of Irish ancestry made up 19 percent of Montreal's English-speaking residents and those who attended Saint Patrick's represented a Who's Who of the city's Irish social register. The 1920's were heady days in Montreal. It was the only major city in North America where it was legal to buy alcohol during the Prohibition era. Tourists flocked to the city for its night life. Illicit after-hours bars known as blind pigs were so widespread even McShane joked about them. He often told the story of the Irish lad in his congregation "who was so fond of animals he became obsessed with a blind pig." Montreal earned a reputation as a wide open town during the roaring twenties, but as Camillien Houde, one of the mayors during the period, quipped, "As long as we keep a good balance between the praying and the sinning, I know Montreal will never sink into wickedness." Houde was right. Ironically, it was during Prohibition that Saint Patrick's enjoyed its strongest support. Neighbourhoods revolved around religious holidays and traditional Sunday observances; all children in the parish who were baptised received religious instruction, and adults practised their faith. Every pew in the church was spoken for.

Saint Patrick's was cleaned for its 75th anniversary in 1922. Dust and grime had discoloured the ceiling and walls and the interior was washed for the anniversary celebrations. The festivities did not take place in March as planned. Ireland was partitioned in January and because the political crisis in the Old Country created a potentially volatile situation among Montreal's Irish community, it was thought best to postpone the church's anniversary celebration until October so they could encompass McShane's 50th birthday and the 25th anniversary of his ordination. The mass on March 17, 1922, the actual anniversary date, was a low key affair. It was celebrated at 8:20 a.m., and was attended by 87-year-old Mary Doutney, who as a 13-year-old had been present at the opening of Saint Patrick's in 1847. She was described as the owner of several properties, someone "who collects her own rents unaccompanied, is an ardent movie fan, plays the piano, knits her own stockings, and makes all her own clothes." The official Diamond Jubilee banquet was held at the Windsor Hotel on October 16, 1922 where McShane recalled Saint Patrick's debt to the "unmeasured generosity, and the noble self sacrifice" of the Sulpicians.

> The names and deeds of St. Sulpice run like golden threads through the warp and woof of the history of Montreal. Their own characteristic humility may endeavour to bedim the shine or dull the glitter that belongs to these strands, but it will persist. And in the present instance it is not too much to say that the Irish people in Montreal never possessed friends more staunch and true. Royal as has been the material assistance given by them in the lifetime of this parish it was most especially in the rare quality of the virtuous and illustrious priests who ministered here that they showed themselves ever to be remembered

benefactors of Saint Patrick's. Simple and eloquent teachers of the truths of religion, wise, prudent and capable administrators, leaders of their people in every move that made for the advancement of these, men of thought and action too, no wonder that Rome, on more than one occasion, sought among them—and not in vain—some upon whom the plenitude of the holy priesthood, the high priesthood of a bishop might be not unworthily conferred.

McShane mentioned Father Jackson, "faithful to the last, a good shepherd to the end," and Father Dowd, for his "simple holiness, his public spiritedness, his many-sided executive abilities, the numerous concrete evidences of his zeal and genius, the practical wisdom of his counselling which made the faithful look up to him as to an oracle."

Quebec presents to the whole Dominion, in fact to the whole continent, a unique and glorious example of peace, order and prosperity. More, in the troubled, distressing critical times through which we are passing, the magnificent economic stability of Quebec bulks large in the esteem of the world and interfering outsiders, prattling disturbers of law and order, temporary demi-gods of unthinking mobs, find themselves absolutely powerless here to lead, in the presence of the cherished traditions of our province, the strength and reverence accorded to the institutions whose influences make their efforts futile.

After the banquet McShane was given a portrait of himself by Adam Sherriff-Scott, which used to hang in the pastor's office until it was removed in 1996. An anniversary booklet published for the occasion in 1922 noted that although the parish limits were becoming "less and less residential, the glamour of Saint Patrick's remains a potent source of influence to its pew holders. Sunday services are still well attended; its mighty throngs are still there."

The church lost one of its most distinguished patrons and benefactors in December 1923 when Lord Thomas Shaughnessy died. Prime Minister

Mackenzie King and members of the federal cabinet attended the funeral on December 13. The prime minister mistook the church for the cathedral, but in his diaries made note of the Fauré *Requiem* which was sung and of the "mass of beautiful floral tributes," which banked the coffin. "The streets were thronged with people, despite the wet weather and it rained most of the way," King wrote. The *Gazette* reporter who covered the funeral thought "the solemnity of the occasion was rendered more impressive by the absolute absence of draping or decoration on the altar itself and in the church. There was a touch of purple on the altar, otherwise it was bare, except for the six candles of high mass and four series of votive lamps each in the shape of a heart. The fine Gothic columns of the edifice remained undraped."

It was the last state funeral to be held at Saint Patrick's.

The floor of the church was tiled in 1925 and the four Austrian stained glass windows were moved to the back of the church. "While the Austrian windows are of good workmanship, they are entirely out of harmony with the beautiful windows made by Locke," was how McShane justified moving them. Two of them had to be cut in half, and the bottom portion of those two windows were saved and put into the sacristy. The last of the Locke-designed windows were added. They depict St. Patrick (with the inset of Father Dowd), St. Michael the Archangel in a window dedicated to "the brave lads of Saint Patrick's who died in the Great War," the Nativity, and St. Bridget of Kildare. Those who support the ordination of women can take comfort from the image of St. Bridgit. She was a high abbess who presided over an Irish monastery that admitted both men and women. Tradition suggests she may have been consecrated a bishop "by mistake" and suggests she celebrated mass, almost certainly heard confessions, and probably ordained clergy. The table grace associated with her name goes like this:

> I should like a great lake of finest ale for the King of Kings /
> I should like a table of the choicest food for the family of
> heaven / Let the ale be made from the fruits of faith and the
> food be forgiving love / I should welcome the sick to my
> feast for they are God's joy / Let the poor sit with us at the
> highest place amid the sick and dance with the angels / God

bless the poor, god bless the sick, and bless the human race!
God bless our food/God bless our drink, All homes, Oh
God, embrace.

The same year the parish acquired a 700-acre site on Lake Castor in
the Laurentians as a summer camp and named it Camp Kinkora.

On December 1, 1926, Richard Key Biggs gave an organ recital. "There
were only three big things, two of them by César Franck, the chorale in B
minor, and the finale in B Flat and Liszt's Prelude and Fugue on the notes
BACH," wrote one critic. "The other things were of a lighter kind."

In the spring of 1927, the noted landscape architect Frederick G. Todd
redesigned the grounds to include St. Bridgit's lawn on the west side of the
church, and a parking lot in front. Todd, who is best known for his work on
National Battlefields Park on the Plains of Abraham in Quebec City and his
layouts for both the Saskatchewan and Alberta legislative grounds, moved
the main entrance gates from the front of the church on La Gauchetière
and relocated them beside the presbytery on Dorchester Blvd., in effect
making the back of the church the front. He also created an attractive system
of serpentine walkways and plantings that meandered around the church
and down the hill. Saint Bridgit's refuge was remodelled and renamed the
Father Dowd Home.

One of the most memorable concerts at Saint Patrick's was held on
Good Friday March 29, 1929, when Dvorak's *Stabat Mater* was performed.
The choir "infused the ancient theme with fresh and poignant meaning ,"
wrote the *Gazette*'s music critic. "The interplay of string and wind
instruments was admirably interpreted on the organ while the glorious
singing proved the choristers to be thoroughly accomplished musicians.
The setting of the sanctuary symbolised the hymn in a most perfect manner.
In the forefront, hiding the high altar completely was a towering cross draped
with a winding sheet. At the base was a beautiful piece of statuary,* the
seated figure of the virgin supporting the lifeless body of her Son as if just

*The statue of the *Pietà* mentioned in the *Gazette* article was unveiled at the performance
to commemorate the signing on February 11, 1929 of the Lateran Treaty by Pope Pius XI
and Mussolini. The treaty guaranteed the autonomy of the Vatican within the Italian state,
and Roman Catholics everywhere were enthusiastic about it. Often mistaken for a copy of
Michelangelo's masterpiece, the *Pietà* remained at the back of the church for more than 50
years until 1996 when it began to crumble and was removed.

taken down from the tree. The space on either side was filled in completely with tall candelabra, Easter lilies in pots swathed with the purple mourning of Holy Week and masses of palms in the background. The church was filled both as to floor and gallery, and many persons were unable to secure seats. Reverend Gerald McShane mounted to the pulpit and extended a special welcome to those who were not members of the church."

Saint Patrick's was now an affluent parish and operated on a grand scale. The organist was paid $1,800 a year, well above the average salary of $25 a week. It was not uncommon for the sacristan to spend $100 a week on floral decorations for the altar at a time when 10 cents could buy what $5 or even $10 does today. McShane had vestments imported from England and France. The church published its own glossy magazine, *Saint Patrick's Messenger*, which went out each month to 5,000 subscribers. The one hundred voice boys' choir was acclaimed as the city's best. When the choir placed first in a CFCF radio competition, the adjudicator who awarded the prize, Herbert Ruel, declared "the exquisite tone of the boys' choir is quite equal to that of the best English choirs; the perfect balance and blending of all parts, the precision and beautiful shading." Choristers were paid 15 cents each for every mass they sang! No expense was spared to make ceremonial occasions as sumptuous as they were sacred. Anyone who walked into the church could not help but be impressed by the extravagance. "It would require a pen of gold to adequately describe the beauty of Saint Patrick's," wrote one visitor who showed up for the 40 hours devotion in 1929. "Stepping into the incomparable Irish church, from the bustle of the busy street, to the dim, veiled beauty of its holy calm, the simple grandeur of its altars and aisles, priceless assets at any time, but enhanced by the magnificence of the main altar decked for the 40 hours of Our Lord, the temple was simply indescribable.

"Hundreds of lilies and white mums, an unbroken screen of verdure through whose trellis work glimmered white vigil lamps, chains of blood-red lights and crowning all, the golden monstrance. It was a heavenly dream."

The idyll was shattered with the stock market crash in October 1929. The Depression began and by 1933 the average wage dropped $8 to $17 a week. There was no state welfare and McShane went to work as a champion of social justice. His efforts were exemplary. He helped to establish the Federation of Catholic Charities to augment the work already being done by the Sisters of Providence who ran Saint Patrick's Welfare Bureau. Children in the parish were given free lunches, and McShane often paid the bill out of his own pocket. He created make-work projects so people could be employed. Interior decorator Guido Nincheri was contracted to redo the interior of the church even though his bid was $7,000 higher than what had been estimated. Nincheri, sometimes referred to as Montreal's Michelangelo, had designed and painted the interiors of more than 50 churches, but when it came to Saint Patrick's he decided he "could not improve upon perfection" and didn't change Locke's design. Two dozen people repainted the church in 1931. The salmon and cream colour scheme was the one Locke recommended, except the shades used by Nincheri were two tones lighter. The same year radio station CFCF suggested McShane deliver a series of sermons on the air to raise money for the poor. McShane used the broadcasts to solicit funds for a number of religious charities, not just Roman Catholic. One of his broadcasts in November 1931 was in support of the Federation of Jewish Philanthropies.

On Sunday, August 7, 1932 Saint Patrick's welcomed the Sulpician superior Jean Cardinal Verdier, the Archbishop of Paris. Verdier, one of the best known clergymen of the era, was a champion of the oppressed and one of the first churchmen to denounce Adolph Hitler who was then gaining prominence in Germany. The day before Verdier arrived in Montreal thieves made off in broad daylight with the 75-foot red carpet that had been laid up the steps. The sacristan saw the carpet disappear around a corner and took off in pursuit. Unable to run with their booty the bandits dropped it in the street and it was in place, none the worse for wear, when the Cardinal arrived to a tremendous welcome.

The Depression squeezed church finances. At their meeting on October 8, 1933 the wardens reported that "receipts were considerably decreasing, owing of course, to the prevailing Depression. Total revenues for 1930 were five percent less than 1929, for 1931, eight percent less, for 1932, 30 per cent less, and for 1933, 27 percent less than 1929. It was the opinion of the meeting that every possible means should be used to meet this condition of affairs and that strictest economy should be exercised in the current expenses." That of course did not stop the ongoing improvements to the church. As part of the continuing effort to make work for the parish, the church was re-wired for electricity and $14,000 was spent in 1933 to replace the slate roof with copper. "The slate roof was a fine piece of work in its day," noted the *Gazette*. "The hand of time, however, wrought its restrictive work. Although the defects were only noticeable in parts … the slate could not be repaired in a satisfactory manner, and the installation of a new roof of solid copper was the most practical course to adopt." The George Reed Metallic Roofing Company employed 14 men to do the work, and their salaries were noted: five men at 65 cents an hour, one man at 60 cents an hour, two men at 40 cents an hour and seven men at 35 cents an hour. A suggestion from the contractor that $900 be spent to apply a saline, soda and potash solution to turn the copper green, was rejected. "The price for washing down and touching up the copper is out of the question," McShane wrote. "We do not want any extras."

The tight financial circumstances did not, however, prevent McShane from going to Europe for two months in1934, the first time he had been abroad since1913. He spent time in Rome and had two audiences with Pope Pius XI, then went to Ireland where he was received by President Eamon de Valera. McShane returned to Canada aboard the *Duchess of Athol*, and like most conservatives at the time, was impressed with Mussolini's Italy. "Italy has certainly changed since the time of my student days," he told a newspaper reporter. "The 12 years of Il Duce's regime have certainly impressed their mark both on the Italian people and upon Rome itself.

"Of course the people have suffered during the Depression like those in all other nations, but the peasants there seem to satisfied with very little. Certainly in the streets of Rome there is no appearance of hardship; the beggars of the old days are not to be seen, the people are exceptionally well dressed, and as for the children, well, they are pictures of good health and contentment.

"If we don't have the historic background of great European cities, we have many things in Montreal the Europeans envy. The absence of the threat of war for one thing, and military rule of law for another."

McGill University conferred an honorary Doctor of Laws degree on McShane in 1936 "for his untiring energy in promoting all manner of charitable and beneficent enterprises." Among those enterprises was his remarkable effort to foster vocations. It was estimated that during the 1920s and 1930s one-third of all the priests in the diocese had been recruited by McShane. "He used to interview every graduating class," said Emmett Carter, "and if he thought someone showed potential, he'd be very direct. 'Have you ever thought about being a priest?' he'd ask. He often paid for their education out of his own pocket if the boy's family couldn't afford it." So capable was McShane, on May 22, 1937 three priests were ordained simultaneously for the first time in the church. Among them was Carter who would go on to become the cardinal of Toronto. Carter celebrated his first high mass in the church on May 30, 1937.

1939 was a pivotal year. Pope Pius XI died in February; King George VI and Queen Elizabeth came to Montreal in May, and McShane attended the civic banquet for the royal couple at the Windsor Hotel. Seated between a rabbi and the Moderator of the United Church of Canada, he quipped, "I'm not here to divide you, I'm here to bring us all together." World War II broke out in September, and two weeks later, Bishop Bruchési died. The stain of war coloured relations between French and English in Montreal. Unlike World War I, however, there was no question about the loyalty of Saint Patrick's parishioners to the Crown. "We may love Ireland," McShane said simply "but we love freedom even more." On February 18, 1942 he introduced a noon mass at Saint Patrick's "so prayers appropriate for wartime" could be offered daily for the armed forces. The conscription crisis erupted in Quebec at the same time and once again, the St. Patrick's Day parade was threatened with cancellation. The organizers held it anyway as a patriotic demonstration, and as "a tribute to Canada's growing military strength as well as to Ireland's patron saint." It went ahead on Sunday, March 15. Soldiers, sailors, and airmen joined firefighters and a group of U.S. soldiers on leave in what was described as the largest St. Patrick's Day Parade ever witnessed to that time. The church was even more crowded than usual for the mass. "Not only was every seat of the nave occupied, but dense crowds stood in the rear and the attendance overflowed into the gallery," reported the *Star*. "Harps and shamrocks outlined in soft green hung from the high altar." That evening, for the first time, a toast to the king was proposed at a United Irish Societies banquet. The reality of war was driven home at Saint Patrick's at the end of October when 16 airmen were killed at Dorval in the crash of an R.A.F. Ferry Command plane. Three of the dead, Bernard Malone from Kirkland Lake, Ontario, Vincent Peebles

of Halifax, Nova Scotia and Michael Casey from Sydney, Nova Scotia, were
buried with full military honours from the church. "The three caskets each
draped in the Union Jack were reverently borne to the communion rail
and a solemn High Mass was chanted for the repose of the souls of these
three Canadian lads who risked their lives in the service of their country."
The *Saint Patrick's Messanger* wrote of the event: "When the solemn rites
were over, 18 young men, brothers in arms of the three crash victims,
proceeded with perfect precision from their pews to either side of the
three caskets. Gently and respectfully these were lifted to shoulder height
and carried down the centre aisle as the great organ rendered its soul-
stirring strains and the bells sounded a last farewell. Each body draped in
the national ensign was carried on a simple motor truck of drab grey. There
was only one regret expressed—the inability of the families of the young
air men to attend the imposing funeral."

McShane was made a monsignor in 1943 and his elevation inspired
both awe and intimidation. Although he still preferred to be called "Father"
instead of "Monsignor" he swayed and sailed magnificently down the aisles
each Sunday morning as he personally took up the collection. "He became
totally predictable, very direct, and very demanding," recalled Emmett
Carter. Carter was McGill University chaplain in the 1940s and had hoped
to hold the students' mass at Saint Patrick's. McShane agreed to the plan on
an trial basis. After several Sundays, however, McShane abruptly withdrew
the offer.

> He sent me in detail a statement of how many quarters,
> how many nickels and how many dimes the students had
> put in the collection plate, and found it wanting. He said a
> student mass at the church wasn't worth the effort, and
> told me to find somewhere else. We went to Sacred Heart
> convent. A few years later when the mass was established
> there, and proved to be popular, he walked me through
> the grounds of Saint Patrick's, and said we should come
> back to St. Pat's. I turned him down. He wouldn't speak to
> me again for years.

For all his apparent public largesse, McShane was parsimonious with his
own curates and cruelly insensitive to his staff. "He never gave his priests

"He seemed like the old building itself."
Msgr. McShane, March 1937.
The last of the Sulpician priests at Saint Patrick's.
Photo by Rice. Courtesy of the Montreal Gazette.

their own keys to the rectory," Carter recalled. "The doors were locked at 11 p.m. and if a priest wasn't in by then he had to find somewhere else to sleep for the night. McShane was very tough. He kept a padlock on the doors to the ice box. He was a powerhouse, but he was tough." After one midnight mass priests returned to the rectory for a *réveillon* only to discover that McShane had retired for the evening and all he had left them to eat was a tin of sardines. "They were lucky to get that," Carter observed.

During the war, a young curate at Saint Patrick's, Father Matthew Dubee, began an amateur theatre group which he called the St. Genesius Players Guild, otherwise known as the Genesians. The company took its name from Genesius, a pagan actor who was given a mock baptism while performing in a burlesque of Christian rites for the Roman Emperor Diocletian. During one performance, however, Genesius departed from the script and proclaimed his faith. Diocletian had him beheaded. The Genesians staged its first play, Henri Gheon's *Christmas on the Village Square* in December 1943, but McShane was not impressed. Plays had been done at the church as early as 1932 when productions of *The Upper Room* and *It's the Climate* were produced, but they were more pageants than dramas. When Dubee's company started tackling contemporary, popular material like the Brandon Thomas farce, *Charlie's Aunt*, *The Constant Heart*, and Tennessee Williams' new play, *The Glass Menagerie*, McShane informed Dubee that the theatre would be the ruin of a good priest. Dubee continued to work under a pseudonym. When McShane found out about it, he had Dubee transferred out of the parish to St. Aloysius in east-end Montreal. Undeterred, Dubee continued to indulge his hobby. He produced the Catholic Hour on CJAD, went on to became a professional magician, was elected a director of the Catholic Theatre Conference in the United States, and for one year was the casting director for the Passion Play staged in the Black Hills of South Dakota. He was also responsible for getting the leading Catholic evangelist in the United States, Bishop Fulton J. Sheen to come to Montreal for a religious rally in the Forum.

When World War II ended in 1945, 197 men from Saint Patrick's had been killed in action. A partial list—those who graduated from St. Patrick's Boys School—hangs in the St. Alexandre street stairwell in Congress Hall. The post-war economic boom was accompanied by social upheaval, and in the aftermath of World War II Montreal and Saint Patrick's were greatly altered. People moved out of the central core of the city and the neigh-bourhoods that had traditionally supported the church quietly died. Much of Little Dublin, the area in the immediate vicinity, was razed during Canadian National Railways redevelopment of downtown Montreal. St. Patrick's school was torn down to make way for the University Street extension. Parishioners moved to the suburbs, and new English-speaking parishes were created in the Town of Mount Royal and on the West Island. Maurice Duplessis was re-elected premier in 1944, and would remain so for the next 15 years. Duplessis was a devout Catholic, and his biographer Conrad Black suggests the political party he founded, the Union Nationale, was patterned after the church: "highly structured, meritocratically ruled, suspicious of elites and social tinkerers." Catholicism during the Duplessis years was pervasive and absolute. Whenever the premier inaugurated a bridge, dedicated a building, opened a power plant, a road or a chicken farm, a bishop in flowing robes was always front and centre.

A bishop was consecrated at Saint Patrick's for the first time on June 7, 1945. The event was noteworthy because Gerald Berry, head of Montreal's Catholic Welfare Bureau was, at 42, not only one of the youngest prelates ever, but was one of the few to be appointed directly from the priesthood to the episcopate. The apostolic delegate Archbishop Ildebrando Antoniutti conducted the service which was attended by archbishops from Regina, Kingston, and Ottawa. Three weeks later Berry, a doctor of sociology, was installed as bishop of Peterborough, Ontario. In 1953 Berry was appointed archbishop of Halifax, a post he held until his death in 1967.

Saint Patrick's observed its centennial in 1947. Three Cardinals—James Cardinal McGuigan of Toronto, Norman Cardinal Gilroy of Sydney, Australia, and Bernard Cardinal Griffin of Westminster, and 50 bishops and archbishops attended the centennial mass on Sunday, September 14. Cardinal McGuigan delivered the sermon: "For 100 years, in fair weather and in foul, in joy and in sorrow, in prosperity and in want, Saint Patrick's of Montreal has raised its gracious tower to the skies in benediction over the tangled pathways of life, a home of celestial peace amidst discordant clamours of the world." The occasion also marked Msgr. McShane's Golden jubilee as a priest, and his 40th anniversary as pastor of Saint Patricks. CFCF radio carried a live broadcast of the service. In his remarks that day McShane likened the church to "a watch tower in the heart of a great city."

With its tapering spire towering above the surrounding buildings, St. Patrick's is symbolic of the greatness and permanence of the faith for which it stands."

Governor General Field Marshall Viscount Tunis was guest of honour at the banquet at the Windsor Hotel the following day.

An unexpected and prominent new parishioner began showing up for mass at Saint Patrick's in 1949—Premier Maurice Duplessis. Whenever he was in Montreal the premier usually worshipped at Mary Queen of the World Cathedral. He stopped doing so after a May Day sermon in which Archbishop Joseph Charbonneau singled out his government for criticism for its handling of a bitter strike by asbestos workers. Charbonneau accused Duplessis of being part of "a conspiracy to crush the working class," and declared that in the interest of social justice the church had a mandate to intervene to end the strike. The premier was accustomed to provocation from the liberal press, but not to such an assault from the episcopate. After that, Duplessis refused to set foot in the cathedral until he had the Vatican remove Charbonneau from office. He started going to Saint Patrick's instead. Even after Charbonneau had been replaced as bishop in 1950 by Paul Emile Léger, another Sulpician, Duplessis frequently showed up at Saint Patrick's. He preferred to sit on the left aisle, in pew number 238, directly below the pulpit.

Archbishop Léger paid his first visit to Saint Patrick's on Sunday March 11, 1951. "We at Saint Patrick's are disciples of tradition. Events in their allotted sequence come and go each year, but the Archbishop's visit seemed to make history with its rich pageantry of sacred rites," the *Messenger* said of the visit. "It mattered not that the sombre air of Passiontide was upon us, and that purple veiled the cross and statues. The richness of the ceremonial took our minds off the usual sadness of the Lenten season. Providence has gifted our Archbishop with a clear tenor voice. The preface and the *Pater Noster* were never sung more impressively. Needless to say, every seat in the church was occupied and there were standers in the rear." Léger used the occasion to talk not about St. Patrick, but about vocations. 1951 marked the first year since 1866 in which no one from the parish was ordained a priest, and the first year that no English-speaking seminarians from Montreal entered the priesthood.

McShane celebrated his 80th birthday in 1952 at the Mount Stephen

Club. He used the occasion to deplore the fact that so few of his parishioners could speak French. "For a city that is supposed to be bilingual, bilingualism is found in relatively few people," he complained. McShane suggested that English-speaking Montrealers learn French not to be assimilated, but rather so "they might be integrated and not be excluded from the social, cultural, religious and economic life of the province of Quebec." In spite of his age he had no intention of retiring. "I am in perfect health, and with God's grace I intend to carry on my duties for some time to come." Although not as robust as he once was, McShane led the last of the parish pilgrimages to Bonsecours Church in Old Montreal in May 1954, and took part in a Pentecost rally in June at Molson Stadium.

Msgr. McShane retired on April 18, 1955. The *Gazette* ran an adulatory editorial headlined, "Father McShane Leaves Old St. Patrick's" and described him as a man "with humanity in his faith, and charity in his deeds. Though he will no longer be pastor, he himself will be in the minds of many, also symbolic of the greatness and permanence of faith in this troubled and anxious world." Six months later, on October 17, he was dead. One radio announcer remarked that it would be hard to imagine Saint Patrick's without him. "He seemed like the old building itself, to be sure to outlast the come and go of the great city." McShane left an estate worth more than $200,000. In his will he bequeathed $2,000 to the Sulpicians to have masses celebrated for the repose of his soul. He left $50,000 to start a trust fund for the education of priests and his summer cottage at Ste. Lucie de Doncaster in the Laurentians went to Camp Kinkora. He willed his books and his art collection "to those may appreciate them—preferably priests." There were various small bequests to his nephew, the Rev. Donald Feron, to his faithful secretary, Eva Johnson, and to other employees. The bulk of the estate, however, went to Saint Patrick's. His body was exposed for two days in the Lady Chapel. Léger, who had by then become Montreal's first cardinal, celebrated the funeral mass in the church and praised McShane for being a great administrator and organiser. "To be responsible for a large city parish and the care of its church and buildings, to see the need for a summer camp for boys, to maintain and improve a home for the aged and the orphaned, these are great works which require skill and ability," said the cardinal.

With that, the last of the Sulpician priests at Saint Patrick's was interred in the crypt of the Grand Seminary on Sherbrooke Street.

Chapter Ten

MCSHANE WAS ALSO THE LAST of the imperial clerics at Saint Patrick's. His successor Harold Joseph Doran was a pale imitation. Like McShane, Doran was a product of his times—an old-fashioned priest in the sense that he lacked imagination, but valued prudence, thrift, determination and perseverance—qualities that earned him respect in the community. The future Canadian prime minister John Turner, who was the English-speaking legal advisor to Cardinal Léger and a warden at Saint Patrick's, didn't consider Doran "a downer" after McShane. "He was a very, very confident administrator," Turner recalled. "There was a great mood around the place when Doran took over, almost like a breath of fresh air. He was a good parish priest in a difficult era."

Doran was born March 16, 1901, the son of a Westmount building supply contractor, James Doran. His uncle had been the architect in charge of remodeling the church in the 1890s. Doran attended St. Patrick's Boys School and the Collége de Montréal before he entered the priesthood in 1922. He was ordained in the cathedral on May 29, 1926, and sang his first high mass at Saint Patrick's the next day. "Considerable interest is being centered on the young clergyman inasmuch as he is a former 'Saint Patrick's Boy," the *Star* reported when he was ordained. "An alumnus of the parish school and of the boys' chancel choir, he has never ceased to be closely identified with the parent church of the English-speaking Catholics of Montreal. A program was arranged for the fitting reception of the young priest on the occasion of his first holy mass. Special music will be rendered by the mens' choir and the boys' choir under the direction of the new organist, R.M. Selby, and the parents of the young priest will occupy places of honour and will receive holy communion at the hands of their son."

Doran was curate at Saint Patrick's until 1938 when he was appointed chaplain of St. Patrick's Orphanage. He served as an inspector for the Catholic School Commission and in1946 was assigned to Annunciation

Harold Joseph Doran became pastor of Saint Patrick's in 1955.
He was made a monsignor in 1957 but was ill-prepared for the
changes that resulted from the Second Vatican Council, 1959-65.
Photo by Garcia Studio. Courtesy of Saint Patrick's Basilica.

parish in the Town of Mount Royal as founding pastor. He remained there until he returned to Saint Patrick's as its pastor on May 1, 1955.

"He left the Church of the Annunciation in tears," Bishop Neil Willard remembered. "He was very upset, he didn't want to take on Saint Patrick's. Doran had a hard time of it at Saint Patrick's, but to his credit he kept the operation going during troubled times."

Shortly after Doran became pastor, the steeple at Saint Patrick's was hit by lightning. Then building contractors discovered the walls were crumbling. For those who believe in such portents it represented an ominous beginning for Doran's administration. An emergency meeting of the board of wardens convened in July 1956 to deal with the situation was told, "that over the years water had seeped between the walls and the pilasters with the result that the winter frost had caused them to crack to such a point that they began to fall. It was further noticed that for the same reason many stones in the walls of the church were very loose and ready to fall, especially under the Rose Window." Repairs costing $16,000 were approved; the contractors estimated that $28,000 more would be needed if the building was to be saved. Doran organized a "Save Saint Patrick's spring fair" to raise money but it wasn't very successful. Wardens were forced to dip into a trust fund to finance the repairs.

Doran was made a monsignor in 1957, but he was ill prepared for the whirlwind of changes about to be unleashed upon the Church when on January 25, 1959 Pope John XXIII announced plans for a Second Vatican Council. The Pope envisioned a second Pentecost, or *aggiornamento*, in which the Holy Spirit would breeze through the Church and permit the Vatican to revise outdated canon laws, reorganize the hierarchy, and bring Church teaching up to date. It was in that spirit of reform that television cameras were brought into Saint Patrick's for the first time on Sunday, March 13, 1960, when the CBC telecast across the country the solemn high mass celebrated by Cardinal Léger.

In July, William Power, who as a boy had sung in the church choir, was consecrated a bishop in a colourful, moving three-hour ceremony at Saint Patrick's that was attended by 3,500 people, including 250 priests from across the country. At the end of the ceremony the newly appointed bishop of Antigonish, Nova Scotia marched in a solemn procession through the packed church where he had been baptized 44 years earlier, and gave his first episcopal blessing. Among those in the audience were the bishop's 81-year-old mother, and his brother, a commander in the Royal Canadian Navy.

Television cameras returned for a second time that year on December 17. "There is a nostalgia about a very old church. One can reach way back into its history," the *Messenger* wrote afterward. "As we look about the church there is height, depth and wide display; there is the ecclesiastical artistry of the altar and its appointments. These things are seldom seen today. On the one hand there is a sense of pride of possession as we view the grandeur of the church. Through the complex and technological media of television, all these things can be shared by thousands far and wide across the whole nation." Television became a pervasive influence. When Pope John XXIII became ill early in 1963 the progress of his illness was followed on TV by millions of anxious people around the world, and when he died in June, television carried the papal funeral live for the first time. TV cameras were there as an eyewitness when the second session of the Vatican Council opened in September, and again when the president of the United States, John Fitzgerald Kennedy was assassinated in Dallas, Texas, in November. Kennedy was the first Roman Catholic to be elected president. His background was Irish and he had worshipped at Saint Patrick's during a visit to Montreal in 1952 when he was still a United States senator. A requiem for the murdered president was sung at Saint Patrick's on Monday, November 25, the day of his funeral in Washington, D.C. "Many wept, and they did not try to conceal their feelings as they attended the mass," the *Star* reported. "There was no sermon, only the clear sound of the voices of Saint Patrick's boys' choir. Women knelt in prayer and wept. So did many men." Doran was "highly edified" because, he noted, more than half of those who assisted at mass for the president received holy communion.

Early in 1964 the first of the reforms brought about by Vatican II started to be implemented. Initially, confusion reigned. Old values were shaken up and every aspect of life in the Church was affected. Torn between exhilaration and dismay, the Church withdrew from schools, hospitals, active partisan politics, and social work. Almost overnight its political and social influence in Quebec diminished dramatically. It is impossible to untangle all of the developments and their causes but the effect on Saint Patrick's was pronounced. Many Catholics stopped going to church simply because they didn't think they had to any more. Others concluded that they could accept or reject any given point of canon law as they chose. When Msgr. McShane died in 1955, 88 percent of all Roman Catholics in the parish went regularly to mass; ten years after his death, it was 46 percent. For many Catholics, Vatican II robbed church ritual of much of its mystery and eliminated a good deal of what was familiar. The concepts of hell, damnation, and mortal sin almost disappeared. Eating meat on Friday was no longer a sin. Priests and nuns discarded their cassocks and habits. The Tridentine mass was jettisoned, and the oldest prayer in Christendom, the Kyrie Elieson was translated into the vernacular. People were no longer required to kneel as they received communion, and they were able to take the host in their hands, something that had never been allowed.

Mass was celebrated in English at Saint Patrick's for the first time on October 18, 1964. It all took some getting used to. Traditionalists who did not want to see the church modernized held Doran accountable for all the changes in the parish. "It would indeed be a lengthy task to catalogue the many reasons which directed the council fathers in their decisions in the new liturgical reforms," Doran said as he attempted to defend what was going on. "Suffice to say that mass in the vernacular is here—and it is here to stay. Time and good will take care of these matters. The liturgy has not lost any of its age-old splendour, in fact it has been ennobled and enhanced in new glories."

Talk of remodeling the church to accommodate new rules requiring the priest to face the congregation caused even more consternation. There were suggestions that the high altar would have to be dismantled. In some churches existing reredos and ornate altars were carted away, or hidden behind drapes; statues were put away, murals erased with white-wash and devotions such as benediction done away with. In February 1965 wiser heads prevailed at Saint Patrick's and the sanctuary was re-arranged and a new altar built in front of the old one without disturbing the esthetics of the original. Then the drift to folk masses began; guitars were used for accompaniment as well as the organ. One disgruntled parishioner complained high mass had become nothing more than "a sing-along around a kitchen table." Doran had to deal with the complaints. On more than one occasion he was compared unfavourably to Msgr. McShane.

"The preceding pastor administered the parish for nearly 50 years," one warden complained. "Now Father McShane was a clever organizer who attended to details. Many of his accomplishments give testimony to his foresight. The present pastor must take into account the numerous customs that are part of this whole parish structure. He will have to adopt them to the transformations that are taking place in this ever growing urban district."

Doran and his peers in the clergy also had to do battle with the rise of secular humanism. In October 1965, for instance, *Time* magazine declared God dead. The newsmagazine argued that Christianity's traditional beliefs were irrelevant as outdated cultural forms, suggesting that the idea of a transcendent God was obsolete. The obituary was premature. God didn't die, but for many believers who went through the permissive atmosphere of the 1960s, it seemed he had gone into hiding. Attendance at mass continued to dwindle. On the short term, the reforms invited neglect; Saint Patrick's lost legions. The church bulletin, *Saint Patrick's Messenger*, which had been published every month since 1913, printed its last issue in December 1965. At about the same time, Msgr. Doran's health began to fail and shortly before Christmas he learned he had cancer. He died on April 2, 1966. The day before the funeral the *Gazette* commented on the loss of "a friend and a leader whose work in the community went beyond that of a spiritual counselor, beyond his own parish and his many duties there." Cardinal Léger celebrated the requiem mass at Saint Patrick's. "Towards his bishop and his diocese he showed a loyalty and understanding which was often a great comfort to me," Léger said in his eulogy. "If these are old fashioned virtues, then we need more old-fashioned priests. Nothing can take the place of loyalty, regularity, and devotion. In all these things, Msgr. Doran has left an example we would do well to follow."

He is buried in the Doran family plot in Notre Dame des Neiges Cemetery.

Chapter Eleven

"But he's not Irish, he's a Scot," was the indignant reaction when some parishioners learned that Bishop Norman Gallagher was to be the eighth pastor of Saint Patrick's. Others were astonished to discover that the bishop had no previous ties to the parish. He was a career officer in the Royal Canadian Air Force, and his entire ministry had been spent in the military. Gallagher was an RCAF wing commander, the first Canadian armed forces chaplain to be consecrated a bishop. He was born May 24, 1917, in Coatbridge, Scotland, one of eight children in a family that emigrated to Canada when he was six-years old. His father was Irish; his mother a Scot. He grew up in Swift Current, Saskatchewan, and was ordained in Gravelbourg on March 29,1941. His first assignment as a parish priest was in the farming community of Gull Lake, west of Swift Current. He had been on the job for only a few months when his bishop enlisted him as a chaplain in the Royal Canadian Air Force. "I was too young to be consulted on the matter," he recalled. "A war was on, the service was short of chaplains, so I went." He was posted to Metz, France. Men who had served with him overseas remembered Gallagher as a matchless story teller. "I never knew there were so many clean funny stories until we got Padre Gallagher," said one pilot. "He did more than attend to his spiritual job ministering to the Catholics; he kept up the spirits of the whole outfit with his gift of humour. He'd always have a tremendous parade of Protestants wishing him joy." When World War II ended, Gallagher was posted to Britain until 1950 when he was named chaplain to the Canadian forces in Korea. When the Korean war ended, he assigned to the Air Force base at St. Hubert, Quebec. in 1954. He was consecrated a bishop in 1963. To his buddies in the service who always saw him in his Air Force blues, Gallagher was known as "the bishop who never wore black." He had worn a uniform most of his life, and his episcopal robes took some getting used to. "They were," he said, "akin to wearing a skirt, which isn't the same as wearing a kilt." Adverse to pretense and bombast, he was appointed as an assistant to the Primate of Canada, Maurice Cardinal Roy in Quebec City. When Msgr. Doran died, Cardinal Léger had Gallagher transferred to Montreal as an auxiliary bishop. "The custom had been for the bishops in Montreal to live in the episcopal palace behind the Cathedral, but Gallagher didn't want that," recalled a colleague, Msgr. George Bourguignon. "Gallagher was a people person. I think he irked the cardinal who wanted him at Saint Patrick's as pastor in name only." Another friend, Bishop Power confirmed the story. "The armed forces was Gallagher's life. He was content where he was, then out of a clear blue sky he landed in La Belle Province. If he requested to be in an English-speaking environment, it was because he didn't want to be the only anglophone in a house surrounded by 20 French-speaking priests and bishops." Gallagher's duties at Saint Patrick's are spelled out in the minutes of the meeting of the board of wardens on October 28, 1966. "In view of the fact that his excellency Bishop Norman Gallagher will be impeded from fulfilling his duties as pastor because of his diocesan duties as Episcopal Vicar and Director of English Language Affairs, Leonard Crowley will function as vicar-co-adjutor and parochial administrator."

The responsibility for running the church on a day-to-day basis was vested with Father Crowley, the 34-year-old product of the blue-collar St. Aloysius parish in east-end Montreal. Crowley was born there on December 28, 1921. His father worked for the railroad. Fluently bilingual, Crowley studied at Externat Classique Sainte-Croix and obtained his B.A. from the Université de Montréal. He was ordained in 1947 by Archbishop Joseph Charbonneau. His first parish, St. Marc de Rosemont, was French-speaking. It was there, he said, that he developed one of the touchstones of his life-long philosophy: "Never kill individual initiative. Let people do whatever they want to do and carry through their ideas without interference. If the person fails in carrying out a project, they will invariably try again, and when they come back for help, encourage them some more, as long as it's not sinful." Crowley obtained a licentiate in canon law from St. Paul's Seminary at the University of Ottawa, and returned to Montreal to work as notary of the Montreal Marriage Tribunal. He started co-ordinating Montreal's English-speaking parishioners in 1962, a task that occupied his attention for more than 30 years. A progressive theologian with a social conscience, Crowley believed in sharing pastoral work with the laity long before

Vatican II. "The church gave a special role to lay people," he once said. "It is not made up only of priests. The lay person can be present in those places where a priest cannot be. When the average person is given responsibilities, they often go further than what you would ask because they have a certain amount of freedom a priest doesn't have."

With Crowley effectively in charge of the administration at Saint Patrick's, Bishop Gallagher was isolated. Two men of very different temperament were being asked to work in tandem. Crowley was pre-occupied with putting the church finances in order and he spent much of his time on administrative matters. Gallagher didn't know the dynamics of the diocese. In the words of one friend, he seemed to be a very lonely in Montreal. His first Christmas at Saint Patrick's was "down and glum," and he spent it in his room by himself. The congregation never really got to know him, which was unfortunate. For in addition to his wicked sense of humour, Gallagher was a very human, very down-to-earth pastor. A sermon he gave during Christian Unity week in January 1967 is typical of his common sense approach to religion. "What Christians of all denominations need greatly today is not so much a renewal of theology as a theology of renewal," he said.

> Our attitude must take on a newness of greater self-denial and unstinted love. We must be gentle in the service of others and have an attitude of brotherly generosity towards them. And the noblest service we can render is to advance the cause of truth: not Roman Catholic truth, nor Ortho-dox, nor Anglican or Protestant, but God's truth. Not who is right, but what is right. For right is truth, and truth, in its ultimate expression is God.

By the summer of 1967 Montreal sparkled with new architecture as the city played host to the world's fair—Expo 67. In sharp contrast to the new buildings on the city skyline, Saint Patrick's loomed like a dark shadow in danger of being extinguished. During Expo the church presbytery was used as a reception centre for more than 100 visiting priests from around the world, but parochial activities that year fell off. Saint Patrick's was clearly in decline, an inner-city parish catering to a transient congregation, many

"But he's not Irish, he's a Scot," was the indignant reaction when some
parishioners learned that Bishop Norman Gallagher was to be the eighth
pastor of Saint Patrick's.
Canadian Armed Forces Photograph. Courtesy of Saint Patrick's Basilica.

of whom had nothing in common with the Irish or French cultures. Eastern
Europeans arrived, then Filipinos, Vietnamese, and East Indians. The church
was quickly losing its traditional congregation. 1968 was the worst financial
year in its history. Sunday collections averaged less than $1,300. The parish
was still solvent because it had a substantial trust fund, but faced with
dwindling attendance and rising maintenance costs, the present was drab
and the future uncertain. An architectural consultant, John Bird, discovered
the south facade badly deteriorated and in need of repair. "The wooden
railing at the base of the belfry is badly rotted and constitutes a definite
hazard," he reported. "The stonework facing has generally deteriorated.
These poor surfaces hold the weather and serve to assist the continuing
breakdown of the masonry face. There are signs of split stonework as well
as large areas needing repointing. The belfry contains large amounts of pigeon
droppings, which in itself is not good, but which also may be covering up
certain defects." Churchwardens sought a second opinion, and after a
cursory examination by another consultant, were told the walls were
structurally sound, but in need of repair. "We suspect strongly if the roof of
this structure disappeared (in a fire say) the walls would remain standing
and probably be quite stable due to their size." But the pilasters which
support the walls were crumbling, and their foundations had shifted four
to six inches out of line. Fire inspectors declared vigil lights in the building
a hazard, and the candles were replaced with electric lights. Repairs to the
church were piecemeal, and done on an *ad hoc* basis. To help finance the
repair work Crowley sold 12,000 square feet of church property in the
northwest corner for $660,000 to Dupont Canada. The Sulpicians, who
originally donated the property to the parish as a site for an orphanage,
promptly claimed $80,000 as their seigneurial share. Lawyers for Saint
Patrick's appealed the assessment and cited precedents. "It has always been
the policy of the Gentlemen of Saint Sulpice to negotiate settlements at an
amount considerably less than that to which they have a legal right," they
argued. The Sulpicians re-considered and reduced their price to $45,000.
One of the significant conditions of the sale to Dupont Canada, however,
was that Saint Patrick's would have final approval of any building plans on
the property planned by the new owners.

Cardinal Léger resigned as archbishop of Montreal in December 1967
and left the city to do missionary work at a leper colony in Senegal. He was

succeeded by Paul Grégoire, a bishop bent on building a more co-operative, less hierarchical church in the diocese. Grégoire relied heavily on Crowley for help. So closely did the two work together that Saint Patrick's came to be regarded within the chancery office as something of a co-cathedral. "Inside the house, Crowley was a peach of a priest," a former secretary recalled. "He brought a tremendous spirit to the parish. But he also made many priests in the diocese jealous and envious of his relationship with Grégoire." Under Grégoire the diocese found itself in the throes of re-organization. There were more downtown churches for English-speaking Catholics than necessary. Several parishes had to be phased out, and a number of churches were either closed or torn down, including St. Ann's in Griffintown. The devotions to Our Mother of Perpetual Help which attracted about 400 people to St. Ann's each Tuesday were transferred to Saint Patrick's on August 26, 1969, and the faithful followed. On balance, though, more people continued to move away. A meeting of the wardens at the end of 1969 observed "a continuing trend of people crossing parish boundaries seeking spiritual comfort in parishes other than their own."

No longer a residential parish, Saint Patrick's became an easy target for vandals. There were small thefts from the presbytery, then someone ripped the brass memorial plaque to D'Arcy McGee from an outside wall in front of the church. The plaque had been unveiled in 1967 and weighed at least 80 pounds. A donated replacement was mounted inside the church on a pillar in the sanctuary to the right of St. Ann's altar. People assumed it marked McGee's tomb so the plaque was later moved to its present location at the back of the church to the left of the main doors. There were other indignities. A derelict hid in the washroom while a mass was being celebrated and after the church was locked broke into the sacristy and tried to steal several chalices. Among them was a valuable sterling silver chalice given to Father Doran in 1959. Hallmarked 1708, it came from an estate in Kilbarron, Ireland, and was probably used in penal days. Curates heard the clinking sound and caught up with the intruder a block and a half from the church. On another occasion, a thief stole a couple of gold chalices and managed to pawn them for $100 at a shop a few blocks away. When the broker, Harold Mendelson, learned the chalices were stolen, he gave them back to the church instead of reporting the sale of stolen property to the police. "We had things stolen from our synagogue and we never got them back," he said, "so I know how the congregation felt. I was just happy to see the church get back its property."

In May 1970, Gallagher left Saint Patrick's to become the Bishop of Thunder Bay, Ontario. By then he had developed the affection and love of the clergy in Montreal and had earned the respect of the Saint Patrick's Societies and the United Irish Society, no small achievement.

Five months after he left terrorists belonging to the Front de libération du Québec (FLQ) kidnapped the British trade commissioner in Montreal, James Cross and Quebec's labour minister Pierre Laporte. Laporte was murdered, and the country was in crisis. Prime Minister Trudeau declared the War Measures Act, an extraordinary piece of legislation that suspended civil liberties. Among hundreds of those arrested under its powers was a 28-year old maverick member of the Saint Patrick's congregation, journalist and broadcaster Nick Auf der Maur. Father Crowley reacted by recommending that a special committee be set up to monitor those jailed. In a sermon, he offered guarded reaction to the political crisis. Although he conceded that special measures had to be taken to assure the security of the state, he was critical of the flagrant abuse of the Act. "Given the exceptional circumstances, it was not possible to enact suitable legislation proportionate and adapted to the situation," he said. "But human justice demands new legislation which will give the state less extensive powers than those contained in the present law."

It was assumed that with his qualities of leadership Father Crowley would succeed Gallagher as pastor. Archbishop Grégoire, however, was impressed with Crowley's work as an indefatigable champion of English-speaking Catholics in Montreal and as long-time advocate for increased participation of the laity, and had other plans for him. Crowley was consecrated a bishop at Saint Patrick's on March 24, 1971, before a capacity crowd that included the mayor of Montreal, Jean Drapeau. Instead of putting Crowley in charge of Saint Patrick's, Grégoire named him director of English Language Affairs for the diocese.*

*Crowley returned to Saint Patrick's as nominal pastor in 1994 just before the present pastoral administrator, Rev. Msgr. Barry Egan-Jones was appointed. Among Bishop Crowley's many contributions to the Archdiocese are the Pillars Trust Fund, which helps finance community services, *The Catholic Times* newspaper, the Catholic Counselling Centre, Nazareth House for AIDS patients, the Catholic Information and Referral Service, and the Christian Meditation Centre. Bishop Crowley was diagnosed with Alzheimer's disease in September 1997, and moved into a retirement residence.

Three decades after Matthew Dubee had been sent to Coventry by Msgr. McShane, Grégoire plucked him from obscurity at St. Barbara's parish in LaSalle, and on June 8, 1971, gave him the responsibility and opportunity suited to his talents: he made him pastor of Saint Patrick's.

Chapter Twelve

MSGR. MATTHEW DINEEN DUBEE was a magician with a flair for the dramatic, a good-humoured evangelist with an infectious smile and a mischievous little-boy expression. He was both surprised and delighted to take charge of Saint Patrick's even if the sumptuous church he remembered was now a magnet for inner-city derelicts. "There are those down on their luck who come each morning seeking handouts, and its congregations at Sunday masses are now scattered with nationalities other than pure-blood Irish," wrote *Gazette* columnist John Fitzgerald. The general assumption was that Dubee had been appointed by the bishop to phase out the parish. The federal government had expressed interest in buying the church for a new office complex and private developers had earmarked the property for an exclusive high-rise apartment building. Although the idea of tearing down Saint Patrick's was discussed, according to Bishop Neil Willard it was never a serious option. "The whole tradition of Saint Patrick's is one of conflict between French and English; that tradition is part of the history of Montreal, part of the fabric. Saint Patrick's has always been a centre of action. It is like a suspension bridge between the two cultures. Tension keeps it aloft. The creative tension is one of the reasons the church is a success story. It would have been unthinkable to tear it down." Father Dubee assured the church wardens he would not preside over the demise of the church. "Our faith is strong, and our parish is not about to disappear," he said. He recognized, however, that more than sentiment was needed to rejuvenate Saint Patrick's. "Dubee started the ball rolling," said Willard. "He put life back into the place that wasn't there under Doran or Gallagher or Crowley. He began to spend money, too."

Dubee was born in Westmount on January 26, 1913, and grew up on Arlington Ave. His father Patrick was treasurer for the Montreal Tramways Company. "His name was on all the street car tickets," Dubee recalled. He attended church at St. Léon de Westmount, and was educated by the

Christian Brothers at St. Leo's Academy. He attended Loyola College where he was captain of both the football and hockey teams, and won a medal as being most representative of the ideal Loyola student. An athlete with a physique, he posed for body-building shots before he entered the priesthood. Even after he was ordained, "all the girls in church went bananas over him because he was so handsome," recalled *Gazette* fashion writer Iona Monahan. Dubee studied social economics at Georgetown University in Washington, D.C. before enrolling for the priesthood at the Grand Seminary on Sherbrooke St. He was ordained on June 7, 1941. When he started the Genesians in 1946, Dubee wrote his own profile for the Genesian's program notes:

> My father is a Saint in heaven; my mother tries to be a Saint on earth, my sister is an angel—in fact she is Sister St. Maureen of the Angels, of the Congregation of Notre Dame. These are the finest things I can tell you about me. Apart from being such a fortunate accident of birth I was subjected to years of RRR, which some understand to mean 'reading, 'riting and 'rithmatic, but which others interpret as ranting, raving and ridicule. My first year as a priest was spent teaching English in a French college, L'Externat Classique de St-Sulpice. Since that time I have been attached to Saint Patrick's Parish, Montreal. I am 33, single, BUT attached.

A stylish romantic with a taste for Old Paar Scotch and appetite for manhattans and cigarettes, Dubee recognized that Saint Patrick's linked past to present to future. He was aware that ethnicity alone would not sustain Saint Patrick's, that it would have to reach out beyond the Irish community. He knew which of the old customs to keep, but also opened the church and made it a hub for community activities as well as a spiritual centre. He started serving coffee after the 11 a.m. mass on Sunday so parishioners could socialize. "He was anything but shy," recalled church warden Dr. Mimi Belmonte. "He was blunt, very open. He said what he thought and let the chips fall where they may, and some people couldn't take it." Dubee brought with him to Saint Patrick's Charles Brocklehurst, a professional interior decorator with an eye for the simple, the classic and the traditional. Brocklehurst had been a parishioner at St. Aloysius and had known Father Dubee for years. Before Dubee invited him to be his sacristan, Brocklehurst had planned to move to New York to work at Saint Patrick's Cathedral.

"When we arrived, the church was a mess, old and run down and falling apart. It was foundering," said Brocklehurst. "What we set out to do was to strike a balance and rejuvenate it. We would take a bit of the best from the Vatican II reforms, keep the best from the past, and come up with a happy medium."

In August 1971 Dubee invited folk singers from the Church of St. Andrew the Apostle in London, Ontario to do a folk mass, and took tentative steps to revive the Genesians by inviting the Buxton High School Players, a touring theatre group from Williamston, Mass., to stage a production of T.S. Eliot's *Murder in the Cathedral* in Saint Patrick's. It would be the first of at least four productions to be presented in the church while Dubee was pastor.

He had the organ rebuilt for the church's 125th anniversary in 1972, integrating the Casavant Organ from St. Anthony's Church. Saint Patrick's had lost its organist and choirmaster when William Doyle retired after 40 years. After Doyle left, the choir disintegrated. Dubee reinstated it.

He invited Bishop Emmett Carter to be the honored guest at 125th anniversary celebrations on Friday, March 17, 1972. In a dinner speech at the Sheraton Mount Royal Hotel the bishop suggested that the biggest challenge Saint Patrick's faced was indifference. "This pile of stones is not a statue, is not just a building, but living tradition," he said. He talked of his own ancestors who came to Canada as immigrants in 1830 from Cork. "If someone had spoken collectively to the Irish people of Montreal and said to them in those days, 'You are immigrants, you are poor, you are politically powerless. What are you going to do with yourselves in this budding city in an evolving and growing country? You have nothing, you are nothing. What are you going to do?' Our ancestors would have answered: 'We are going to build a church, and we are going to call it after St. Patrick.'"

Carter reminded his audience that the Irish didn't build the church themselves. "It was faith that built this church and carried it as a living symbol in an increasingly secularized world. Your enemy today is indifference

Msgr. Matthew Dineen Dubee wanted to bring new blood into the church.
He realized that ethnicity alone would not sustain Saint Patrick's—it would
have to reach out beyond the Irish community.
Photo by Max Sauer. Courtesy of Saint Patrick's Basilica.

and worldliness. Whether you are to be worthy of the challenge does not depend on these stones, however beautiful. It depends on your faith, and on your heart."

One week later on April 23, the former pastor Bishop Gallagher came from Thunder Bay to celebrate an anniversary mass. The move to the Lakehead had rekindled his spirits, and in the words of one colleague, "He came up out of the well. He lit the place up with his brightness." *

The 125th anniversary program ended with a mass celebrated on March 4, 1973 by Bishop Alex Carter, the bishop of Sault Ste. Marie, Ontario who had been an altar boy at the church in the 1920s, and with an organ recital on March 13 given by Gerald Wheeler, organist at Christ Church Anglican Cathedral.

On November 11, 1973, Dubee brought the mass in Latin back to Saint Patrick's. He had experimented with the liturgy and the vernacular, celebrating the occasional mass in Gaelic and in French. The Latin mass proved to be so popular that on October 20, 1974, he decided to offer it permanently every third Sunday. The tradition continues to this day. The Tridentine Rite in Latin which had been used since 1542 had been abolished by the Vatican, but there is nothing to prohibit the use of Latin itself. "Many people cannot forget the dignity, splendor and beauty of the great Latin musical works which cannot be or have not been adapted to other languages," Dubee explained. "For these people, the Latin mass is so much a part of their lives they have never been able to accept completely the liturgy said in the common language of the people. The church must follow the modern liturgy because it permits us to participate actively. In large cosmopolitan centres it is good to celebrate the occasional Latin mass because it gives people a feeling of the universal strength of the Roman Catholic Church."

Saint Patrick's was desecrated in the spring of 1974 when a mental patient took a hammer to more than a dozen statues in the nave that had just been reconditioned and lopped their heads off. Since they duplicated saints already depicted in the wainscotting they weren't replaced. Although he expressed dismay at the vandalism, privately Dubee thought the statues

*During his visit to Montreal, Gallagher was diagnosed with Parkinson's Disease. His health deteriorated rapidly and he died of cancer on December 28, 1975. At Gallagher's funeral the Bishop of Antigonish, William Power, eulogized him as a priest who had a "sort of sixth sense about the capacity of humans to be sinners and saints at the same time." Bishop Gallagher is buried in Thunder Bay in Mountain View cemetery.

were rather kitsch. "I didn't like them much anyway," he told the sacristan. Dubee wanted to bring new blood into the church, but was hamstrung by government legislation which prohibited anyone from outside the parish to sit on the board of wardens. The problem was that most of the talented people who were willing to serve no longer lived downtown, and therefore, under the *Loi des fabriques*, were ineligible to serve even if they volunteered. So in the spring of 1974 the Quebec legislature amended the law and approved Bill 110, which allowed Dubee to recruit wardens from anywhere in the Archdiocese of Montreal.

Pastors of Saint Patrick's have always recognized the goodness of other faiths, and Dubee was no exception. He brought people into the church without prejudging them or demanding conformity. He approached actress Ginger da Silva to appear in a production of *Our Town*, and when she told him she wasn't a Catholic he cast her anyway. Two productions later, she was Mary in an Easter pageant. "I always thought of Father Dubee as Spencer Tracy," she said. "He had that crusty warmth that Tracy always brought to his priest roles. He loved to make scenery, he was forever painting and cutting and sawing. The lighting and sound, too." He wasn't afraid to experiment. He opened the doors of the church to Dr. Alexander Peloquin's 40-voice chorale from St. Peter and St. Paul Cathedral in Providence, Rhode Island and to a three-manual touring organ nicknamed Black Beauty. The choir, according to one critic, offered a "classic approach to sacred music, with elements of folk, rock, jazz and pop, to create a sound that is very much of today." The Vancouver Bach Choir sang at the church in July, 1974, but Eric McLean, the *Star*'s music critic, was not impressed. "Music and Saint Patrick's church are not comfortable with each other," he declared. "Some choirs might revel in the quintupled echo that causes vocal lines to fuse and words to blur, but the Vancouver choir has no need for such acoustical disguises. The works that came through most beautifully were the Schutz motet, 'Verba Mea Aubribus Percipe,' and the beautiful 'Missa Brevis' of Buxtehude, but then, both of these composers were accustomed to design their music for cavernous spaces."

Inspired by the liberation theology being preached in Latin America, the 1970s gave rise to a new militancy in the church. Saint Patrick's got a taste of it when Brazilian Archbishop Helder Pessoa Cámara of Recife, Brazil, a popular hero with the Catholic left , came calling the first Sunday of February 1975. Cámara, known as the "Red Bishop" because of his radical views, was an eloquent spokesman for the world's poor. His sermon at Saint Patrick's was a direct attack on the rich and on the capitalist system which Cámara claimed oppressed two-thirds of humankind. Rather than sympathize with the poor and the oppressed, he said Catholics were obliged to struggle with them for justice, and that those who failed to do so were guilty of sin by omission. "Is it true or not," he asked, "that at least in origin and in name, it is the small Christian world minority that unjustly holds in oppression, in bondage, in hunger, millions of sons of God, both in poor countries and in the poverty pockets of rich countries?

"Without ignoring the benefits of yesterday and of today, without ignoring the beneficial contributions of the various Christian denominations, it seems evident to me that it is fundamental for us Christians to help overcome communitarian sins and attempt to change the unjust structures that leave two-thirds of humanity in a sub-human condition." Dubee's reaction to Cámara's sermon was perhaps typical. "The bishop," he said "may be a bit of a demagogue, but he's a fabulous man."

The 1970s also marked a growing appreciation in Montreal of the spiritual value of the city's architectural treasurers. In the rush to build for Expo 67 a number of historic properties had been demolished, and residents watched with growing dismay as the trend continued. Activists were galavanized when the magnificent Van Horne Mansion on Sherbrooke Street fell to the wreckers' ball in 1974 to make way for yet another nondescript office tower. A citizen's heritage group called Save Montreal was founded. It prepared an inventory of sites it wanted protected under the Cultural Properties Act. Among them was Saint Patrick's. Dubee was skeptical. He was partially miffed because he hadn't been consulted about the group's intentions, and at the same time he was wary of government interference. "There is no chance Saint Patrick's will be torn down," Dubee argued. "Such a classification means having your hands tied. You actually get very little money from the government. It comes down to the point that you become some sort of ward of the government. You have to get government permission for anything you want to do to the building. The experience in England shows that as soon as a church is declared a historical site or monument it ceases to be vital. It becomes a museum." He also felt that as an a minority English-language institution, the church would be overlooked by Quebec government ministries. Save Montreal's executive committee was not so easily dissuaded. "Parishioners do not stop going to a church because the government has found it to be of historical and architectural interest; witness Europe's renowned churches, protected by government and still active places of worship," they responded. "While we agree that the government financial assistance to owners of classified buildings is far from adequate, we believe this type of protection is a necessary step at present." Worried about the precarious position of the church, the group conceded that "as a tax-exempt institution, the church would not benefit from the 50 percent reduction in taxes given classified non-commercial properties, but it would be eligible for financial help for repairs. The chief advantage is the guarantee that the building be retained for the community."

With the election of the separatist Parti Québécois provincial government in 1976 parishioners were fraught with anxiety. For the first time Quebec had a government committed to independence, and the congregation worried about its place in a militant French-speaking nationalist society. It was left to Bishop Crowley, as head of English Language Affairs for the diocese, to put the political developments into perspective. "While the great majority of the faithful at Saint Patrick's are loyal Canadians, there may also be Quebec sovereignist elements," he said. "There is a variety of political opinion, but there is only one church. It is important that, whatever the outcome, English-speaking Catholics assert their presence, and assert it forcefully, continue to build and preserve their own institutions, and maintain their rightful place in Quebec." Ironically, in the long run, the PQ proved to be more beneficial to Saint Patrick's than other levels of government. "Selectively, the PQ decided which English-speaking institutions it would support, and Saint Patrick's was one of them," said Bishop Neil Willard. "The PQ were trying to buy the English as much as they could, and they recognized that Saint Patrick's had political clout. St. Patrick's is the biggest English-speaking parish in the province. If you extrapolate the French from the archdiocese, it was, back then, the fourth largest English-speaking diocese in Canada, after Toronto, Hamilton, Ottawa, and Vancouver. The PQ certainly recognized the value of the building as an important part of Quebec's *patrimoine*, and perhaps were more sensitive to its historical importance than others who take it for granted." It also didn't hurt that the PQ's Minister of Culture responsible for historic properties, Louis O'Neill, was a French Hibernian, a former Roman Catholic priest of Irish heritage.

The spectre of Quebec separation coincided with renewed civil unrest in Ulster. In 1976 more than 900 bombings were reported in Northern Ireland and 300 people were killed as a result of sectarian violence. Ireland never far from Dubee's thoughts. On November 27, the Peace Movement of Northern Ireland held a rally in London, and two weeks later, the minutes of the wardens meeting reveal that "Father Dubee is in the process of organizing help for Northern Ireland. Hopefully funds will be raised and financial help sent to the proper authorities and used to promote peace." There are no records, but Dubee is thought to have raised at least $20,000 which was contributed to the peace process.

1978 was the year of three Popes. Paul VI died on August 6, and was succeeded by John Paul I, who died after a month in office, the shortest papal reign in modern history. He was followed by the present Pope John Paul II. Twice that summer, Saint Patrick's went into an eight-day period of mourning. At the mass for John Paul I, Bishop Crowley remarked, "The death of a pope is like the death of any other man. Death brings home the meaning of life. It shows us how tenuous life is for all of us." The point was driven home more brutally that summer when Lord Mountbatten of Burma was assassinated. His yacht was blown up by terrorists off Mullaghmore, Ireland on August 27. A memorial mass for Mountbatten at Saint Patrick's was announced, but old suspicions and resentments of the British haunted the service. Just before the service was to begin an anonymous caller threatened to blow up the church if it went ahead. The bomb squad was called in, the building evacuated, but no explosives were found. Mass was celebrated as planned, but the cross bearer was so distraught he refused to walk down the aisle in the episcopal procession

Saint Patrick's welcomed home her most illustrious son, Emmett Carter, on Sunday, October 21, 1979. Carter had been made a cardinal that year by the new pope. In a speech to a banquet that night attended by Montreal's Mayor Jean Drapeau, Carter talked about the changes in Quebec in the 18 years since he had left Montreal. He reminisced about the institutions which the church had laboriously built up through the '30s, the '40s, and the '50s, that had either been dismantled or had undergone radical revolution.

"The St. Joseph's Teachers' College is no longer independent." he said. "The position of the English Catholic minority in the Montreal Catholic School Commission has changed vastly under the impact of PQ legislation (Bill 101), and Loyola College is absorbed into a new unit of Concordia University." Addressing the new political reality in Quebec, Cardinal Carter reminded his audience that English-speaking Quebec Catholics were a minority twice over. "Historically, the education rights of the anglophone Protestant minority were well protected by the British North America Act and its measures were well respected by the francophone majority even to the point of adding privilege to rights," he said, "But legally, the English-speaking Catholic majority have no status and do not really exist as a distinct unity. We depend on goodwill and fairness on the part of our francophone fellow citizens." Having said that, he reassured them that they were not about to disappear.

"You cannot be legislated out of existence unless you allow yourselves to be legislated out of existence," he said.

Cardinal Carter was an obvious person to invite to help raise the profile of the church, but some of Dubee's tactics to revive Saint Patrick's were perhaps overzealous. There were complaints that he exceeded the bounds of decency in January 1980, when he allowed the McGill Faculty of Medicine Refugee Fund to stage a benefit concert for Vietnam War refugees. The evening began innocently enough: mezzo soprano Victoria Grof made her Canadian debut and the Tudor Singers of Montreal sang motets, carols, madrigals, and folk songs. But eyebrows were raised when ballet dancers Karen Kain and Frank Augustyn performed the pas de deux from *Le Corsaire* in the sanctuary. Kain was in a diaphanous gown, and there were audible gasps as Augustyn carried her in a straight arm lift up the steps to the altar. The concert was a success and cleared $14,000, but Dubee had his knuckles rapped for permitting it. But those who disapproved were quick to forgive. *Gazette* theatre critic Pat Donnelly, a member of the congregation, recalled that as Dubee grew older he continued to charm. "He was a very good preacher," said Donnelly. "He could bring tears to your eyes. He wasn't fire and brimstone, but very sentimental. He had a natural sentimental delivery that was very touching, very moving, all the more so as he became older and weaker."

In 1980 the Quebec government called a referendum to decide whether the province would continue to remain within the Canadian confederation. In a pastoral letter read from every pulpit the Catholic Bishops of Quebec endorsed Quebec's right to determine its own political future. At the same time, they reminded parishioners that bishops could no longer engage in politics, and would not tell Catholics how to vote. Church regulations governing the behaviour of the clergy were changed in 1978 to forbid priests from running for or holding political office or engaging in political activities. "Separatism may be treason, but to be a separatist is no sin," Dubee told one anxious parishioner. "We just take it for granted that 95 percent of those who come to Saint Patrick's are Canadians. So what's the point in telling them how to vote?" In the October referendum, the separatist option was defeated.

Pope John Paul II appointed Father Dubee a monsignor in 1981. "To those outside the church, the priest is not quite human, to some inside the church priest are all too human, but the priest is a mystery," Dubee said at the time. "Mercifully, I am not left alone with my unworthiness. I have the whole galaxy of saints in heaven with me."

That year Msgr. Dubee moved the Christmas Eucharist from its traditional midnight hour to 9 p.m, to make it more convenient for suburban commuters from the West Island, the South Shore and Laval to attend. Pew rentals were abolished in 1983. In the three years before the referen-dum, 70,000 English-speaking Roman Catholics moved away from Quebec; More than 600 companies relocated their corporate head offices to Toronto. The exodus had a pronounced effect in every English-speaking parish on the island. Of the 347 pews in the church, only 95 were still spoken for. Although people paid to reserve pews for their families, most of the time they didn't come to church and use them. Rows at the front were almost always empty. Occasionally, when pew holders did arrive to claim their seats, there would be strangers sitting in the pews they had reserved for themselves. The policy was more trouble than it was worth. The wardens agreed that "due to the lack of ushers it was difficult to hold the pews for their proprietors, and that was the cause of some embarrassment to worshippers, it was best to abolish the practice."

Pope John Paul II came to Montreal in 1984, but his schedule was so tight it didn't permit a visit to Saint Patrick's. The sanctuary furniture from the church, however, was loaned for the pope's mass at Jarry Park. A brass plaque on the back of the celebrant's chair identifies it as the one used by the pope during the service; the altar in the Lady Chapel is similarly identified as the one used by the pope.

In October 1985, the highly publicised death from AIDS of actor Rock Hudson signalled the emergence of a worldwide health crisis. The AIDS epidemic became palpable. Although some were quick to claim the disease was God's just punishment for decadent homosexual behaviour, Saint Patrick's resident bishop, Leonard Crowley, would have none of it. He was the first Canadian bishop to celebrate a mass for homosexuals at a gay national conference in Montreal. "If God has made you different, he has given you gifts," he told his largely homosexual audience, and urged them "to accept themselves, and to love as a child of God."

That autumn of 1985, Msgr. Dubee was diagnosed with a kidney ailment, and he resigned as pastor. "Saint Patrick's will always be in his debt," said warden Dr. Mimi Belmonte. "He brought back the ceremony. He promoted the church in a secular world. He worked hard to bring back decorum, dignity and the pageantry that had been missing."

Weeks after Dubee resigned the PQ's Minister of Cultural Affairs, Gérald Godin, declared Saint Patrick's a Quebec historic monument on December 10, 1985.

Chapter Thirteen

MATTHEW DUBEE laid the foundations for the revival of Saint Patrick's, but it was Russell Breen who restored it. Breen was 60. His life had been spent as an academic. He was recovering from a heart attack, and had hoped to be put in charge of a remote, working-class parish.Facing retirement, he dreamed of ministering to a small congregation. Instead, he found himself in charge of Saint Patrick's. Soon after he arrived Breen was made painfully aware of its crumbling tower, cracked windows, and ailing roof. So in June 1986, he commissioned an architectural firm, Werleman & Guy, to do a feasibility study. The firm submitted a 34-page report which concluded that structural problems were so serious the facade of the church needed to be rebuilt. "The stonework around the bell tower is in doubtful shape," the architects discovered. "The north face has a minor crack and the west face extremely serious cracking.The condition of the stained glass windows is uneven—a few are in fairly good condition, and two or three are in bad condition with almost immediate danger. Some windows are split, many have been buckled by the effect of wind and more recently by hot air build-up between the two glazing systems. A considerable amount of lead has dried out." Their prognosis: $2.1million in immediate repair work. The board of wardens accepted the report as information but didn't fully appreciate the urgency. "We thought someday we'd find the money to do it," recalled warden Don Mooney. "We said it would be a good idea down the road, someday when we could afford it. One month after we tabled the report, a chunk of stone fell from the belfry and almost hit and killed a man walking into the church to plan his wedding."

Msgr. Breen concluded that if Saint Patrick's was to be saved, the church could no longer afford to take half measures. He launched a comprehensive $5 million restoration program. The undertaking filled him with anguish and exhaustion, and eventually crippled his health, but not before the job was completed.

Professional fundraisers, Ketchum Canada Consultants, were hired to organize the fundraising campaign. "The biggest obstacle for Father Breen to overcome was that, as a parish priest, he didn't feel comfortable begging for money during a severe economic recession. He worried a lot. He didn't want to know where the money to restore the church was going to come from," recalled Bruce Daze, the consultant in charge of the campaign. "His influence among the corporate elite in Montreal was a significant factor. The parishioners themselves didn't contribute all that much, but the people who did take out their chequebooks and respond positively, did so because of Breen's personality. People responded more to Breen than they did to Saint Patrick's."

Russell Whitton Breen was born in Montreal April 20, 1925, the fifth in a family of four boys and three girls who were raised in the east-end anglophone parish of St. Aloysius. The Breen's traced their ancestry to Wexford, Ireland. Breen's father was a stevedore at the Port of Montreal. Breen studied arts at Loyola College, theology at Université de Montréal and at the Grand Seminary. He was ordained by Cardinal Paul-Emile Léger on June 3, 1950, and celebrated his first mass at Saint Patrick's where he spent his first 10 months as a clergyman. At the age of 26 he was named Roman Catholic chaplain at McGill University, a position he held off and on for 14 years. He also served as national chaplain of the Canadian Federation of Newman Clubs. Breen received his Masters degree in Philosophy from Fordham University in New York and obtained his doctorate in religious studies from the Université de Strasbourg in France in the early '60s where he wrote a thesis on the Anglican theologian Charles Gore. More than a scholar, Breen was a vigorous man who enjoyed skiing, boxing matches, and was a loyal fan of the Montreal Canadiens. When Father Breen came back to Montreal in 1968, he taught ecumenical theology at the Université de Montréal before joining the faculty at Loyola College. At Loyola he served as assistant dean, then dean of arts. When Loyola merged with Sir George Williams University in 1974 he became Dean of Arts and Science and in 1978, Vice-Rector Academic, a position he held until 1985. He was pivotal in the negotiations between Loyola and Sir George Williams University that led to their merger into Concordia University. Breen often remarked that until he came to the basilica his only pastoral work had been as an academic and as a university chaplain. "My years at McGill taught me young people are not apathetic about religion. That morality is on the way up. That people are concerned about the rights of others," he said. "More people will be committed to the Church to the extent that the Church concerns itself with renewal. In the past organized religion went to extremes in promulgating rules."

Breen was made monsignor in 1981. Three years later he had a heart attack and had hoped to retire. When he was named the ninth rector of Saint Patrick's in 1985 he took a sabbatical to prepare for the job; in the interim, Neil Willard served as parochial administrator.

Tall, towering, and tenacious, Breen took over on January 1, 1986, and before the year was out was committed to rebuilding the church. As the magnitude of the job became apparent he was under constant stress, and was often heard to declare, "Oh, my God!" He wasn't praying. The professional fundraisers found that because Saint Patrick's was hidden behind a veil of asphalt and unlandscaped growth, its image in the community had suffered. An initial public survey determined that most people couldn't identify the building. A cross-section of opinion was discouraging. "We've got the cathedral, why do we need Saint Patrick's?" was a common reaction. Said another: "Saint Patrick's will have to contend with its image of an old, monied Catholic church, and confusion as to how it has been allowed to get into such a sorry state." Another suggested: "If you could pick Saint Patrick's up and turn it around, it would enjoy the same kind on notoriety as St. Patrick's on Fifth Ave. in New York City." Still, in spite of the negative comments, the consultants determined that the objective was indeed attainable but would require "a high degree of sophistication and effort on the part of St. Patrick's church and all those individuals in the external community who the church attracts to its campaign team. In particular, Saint Patrick's will require influential and committed opinion leaders from the Montreal community to promote its historic preservation cause." Breen tapped Francis Knowles, the president of Power Corporation, to head the corporate gifts division, and persuaded Brian O'Neill, vice president of the National Hockey League, to serve as campaign chairman. O'Neill agreed to serve because he and Breen had attended Loyola College together. Don Mooney, a retired Shell Canada executive and warden of the church, volunteered to act as project administrator. Mooney's brother was a priest; he and Breen had been seminarians together.

Quebec's education minister Claude Ryan, another French Hibernian, launched the capital campaign on September 20, 1988. Breen was the first to contribute. He pledged $25,000 from his salary over five years. The fund raising campaign took three years and raised 2.8 million, but eventually 706 corporate donors, including theMcConnell Family Foundation, contributed $1.6 million; 58 families among them gave $425,000. Some money came from out of the blue. Eva Johnson, who had been Msgr. McShane's secretary in the 40s and 50s, died and left $100,000. Senator John Lynch-Staunton, a former city councillor and Montreal executive chairman made a substantial donation. Another city councillor, Nick Auf der Maur, pledged the increase in his salary to pay for a window. Former Prime Minister John Turner, who hadn't lived in Montreal for 20 years, gave $5,000,and Charles Bronfman and his wife donated money. A plaque at the rear of the church lists the names of more than 100 of the principal donors.

"We started renovations immediately so anyone in the vicinity knew we were going ahead with this, come hell or high water, and that encouraged people to see their donations were going to a work in progress," said Bruce Daze. First, sections of the bell tower were dismantled and rebuilt. The limestone walls were repaired. On March 17, 1989, the Vatican invested Saint Patrick's as a minor basilica. The term means "royal house," and the title is bestowed by the pope on a church in recognition of its "antiquity, dimensions or fame," but only if its interior satisfies "the esthetic needs of the Christian spirit." For the next two years the interior was disfigured by 70 tons of scaffolding, a reminder that the infirm church was undergoing major surgery. The walls and artworks were stripped of a century of grime. The stained glass in the windows was remounted and the lighting system improved. Throughout the entire process, the mass schedule was not disrupted. When the apse was being renovated and the high altar reconditioned, services were held at the back of the nave; when the back half of the church was under repair, the congregation gathered in front.

Because Saint Patrick's was a historic monument, under Quebec government regulations it qualified for a government subsidy worth 60 percent of approved renovation costs, or about $2 million. "We were all banking on the 60 percent subsidy, when, suddenly and without warning, the government arbitrarily cut the subsidy to 40 percent," Mooney said.

"Although the rules and regulations are there, dealing with the Ministère des Affaires culturels was tough. In the end, Quebec came through with $1.6-million, about $400,000 less than we had expected." To the frustration of everyone involved, the federal government didn't contribute a cent. Breen had expected some assistance from Ottawa. The prime minister at the time was Brian Mulroney and Saint Patrick's, his parish church in Montreal. "All we got from Ottawa," Breen complained, "was a lot of promises, promises, promises."

Project architect Fernando Pellicer said replacing the floor was the biggest headache. "There were a number of challenges, but the floor was the most significant," he said. "We had to replace a linoleum floor that had been installed in the 1920s. We could have gone vinyl, wood, marble, granite, or porcelain ceramic, and we decided on ceramic because of its greatest cost-benefit to maintain. It is the perfect product, but how do you make it not look like a shopping mall? How do you lay it on a wooded deck that's 150 years old? It was not easily done." The floor was designed twice, and the tiles were custom made and imported pre-cut from Switzerland. 40,000 high tempered custom made screws were used to anchor the floor and a rubber membrane was stretched over it before the tiles were laid. The pews were reconditioned and every seventh row of pews removed to give worshippers more leg room.

While the church was being renovated, Cardinal Grégoire paid a farewell visit in March 1990, two years before his death. Father Dubee celebrated the 50th anniversary of his ordination in 1991 and was honoured with a mass on April 7. When a parishioner inquired about his health, the former pastor quipped "M.D. is well, really well, but the old house in which he lives is crumbling." He went into Saint Mary's hospital soon afterwards but didn't lose his sense of humour. "Dialysis is a lot like what we priests do, although they do it physically and we do it spiritually," he said. "They connect me to the machine and cleanse me of impurities. That's what we do in the confessional. They put me on a diet and try to keep me healthy. As a priest I offer the body and blood of Christ at the eucharist. And then as priests we try to preach a good homily and leave people with a good message, so people will live a good life. In the hospital, the nurses are always after you to live as close to a healthy life as you can." Msgr. Dubee died on January 24, 1993 two days before his eightieth birthday. His funeral was held in the

Msgr. Russell Breen believed that if Saint Patrick's was to be saved,
half-measures would no longer suffice. He launched a
comprehensive $5 million restoration program.
Photo by Gordon Beck. Courtesy of the Montreal Gazette.

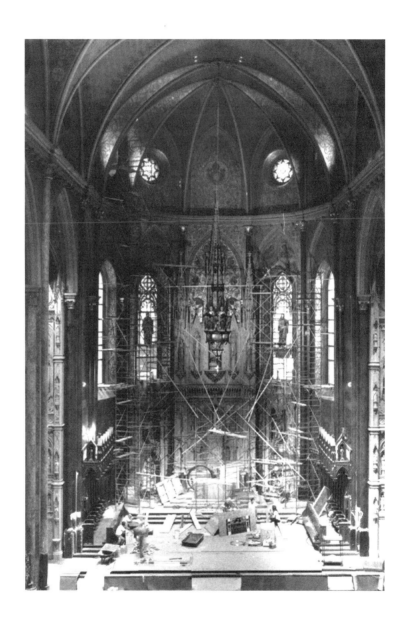

Saint Patrick's Basilica under renovation, July 1991.
Photo by Marie-France Coallier.

Lady Chapel. He is buried the family plot in Notre Dame des Neiges cemetery.

On May 30, 1993, the restoration was completed. To the thunderous strains of Saint Patrick's "Sonata for Four Trumpets and Organ," composed especially for the occasion by Robert Frederick Jones, 700 invited guests celebrated. The sonata was one of three pieces commissioned for the benefactor's service. Jazz musician Denny Christianson contributed "Praise Him," inspired by Psalm 150, and Steve McManaman, the basilica's music director, wrote a contemporary work for four trumpets, "The Spirit Moves Softly on the Souls of Gentle Creatures." After the concert, Archbishop Jean-Claude Turcotte and Monsignor Breen unveiled a bronze plaque to commemorate the restoration. Liberal MNA Jacques Chagnon told the parishioners that the Ministry of Cultural Affairs subsidized the project "not only because Saint Patrick's is one of the most magnificent churches in downtown Montreal, but because it represents our history, our culture."

All those present could not forget the previous Christmas Eve eucharist, when the scaffolding was first dismantled, and they could see the results for themselves. To the surprise and delight of everyone present that December 24th night, Msgr. Breen delivered his homily from Bourgeau's pulpit, which is now only used on ceremonial occasions. It was the same pulpit from which he preached his first sermon 42 years before. "Saint Patrick's", he said, was "an instrument for the divine and human to meet," and he welcomed "especially those who have come from another country and even from another continent for making the basilica more truly catholic." In the tradition of the place, he extended a warm welcome to those "that may not be of our faith or of our parish."

Then he told the story of a woman whose spirit had recently been restored when she walked into the renovated church. He quoted from a letter she had written: "For the last six or eight months my relationship with our Lord had numbed. I had been sick with a virus, and was not able to overcome my illness. I was in fear of prayer, of people, the outside world. I awoke one morning thinking of the interior of Saint Patrick's, of how dark it was. I was dark like that. My husband suggested we go for a drive, and we arrived at the basilica. I did not question our being there. But when I walked in I was astonished. A sense of light sprung up in me. I looked around at the familiar sights, the beautiful stained glass windows, the stations of the cross. I felt the light. Darkness had been replaced with light."

The refurbished church glowed with spiritual brightness, a transcendent statement of English-speaking Roman Catholic culture in Montreal. As he ended his homily, Breen trumpted the words of the prophet Isaiah: "People who have walked in darkness have seen a great light; those who lived in a land of deep darkness, on them a light has shone." The light has been rekindled, and as Saint Patrick's faces the challenges of the next century, it is not about to be extinguished.

Appendix One

The Coat of Arms of the Basilica

Saint Patrick's was made a Canadian National Historic Site in 1997 and the same year the Canadian Heraldic Authority granted the basilica its own armorial insignia.

The green Gaelic cross on a field of gold symbolizes Christ's divinity and divides the crest into four quarters.

At the centre of the Gaelic cross is a smaller St. Andrew's cross in red which represents the City of Montreal.

The basilica's distinctive tower is represented in the shield's upper left hand quadrant.

Papal keys, the Harp of Ireland, and the emblems of Canada and Quebec—the Maple Leaf and Fleur-de-Lys—are featured in the blue bar running across the top of the insignia.

The umbrella represents in miniature a commander's field tent, and placed above the arms indicates that Saint Patrick's church is a basilica. On top of the umbrella is a gilt copper cross. The red and gold stripes of the umbrella are the colours of the Roman Senate in ancient times.

Should the pope visit, a similar striped canopy would be held over his head as he walked into the building.

Appendix Two

Pictorial Litany of the Saints in the wainscotting, beginning from the northwest corner of the church.

COMMUNION OF THE SAINTS
Blessed Virgin
St. Ann
St. Gabriel
St. Marguerite d'Youville
St. Raphael
St. Peter

MEMORIAL PLAQUE TO FOUR FORMER PASTORS
St. Andrew
St. John
St. James the Less
St. Bartholomew.
St. Simon

FIRST STATION OF THE CROSS
St. Mathias
St. Luke
St. Lawrence
St. Thérèse of Lisieux

EDWARD MURPHY MEMORIAL ALTAR
Infant Jesus of Prague
St. Sebastian
St. Monica
St. Augustine

SECOND STATION OF THE CROSS
St. Jerome
St. Martin of Tours
St. Patrick

CONFESSIONAL
St. Columban
St. Lawrence O'Toole
St. Pius X

THIRD STATION OF THE CROSS
St. Golman
St. Mungo
St. Henry

DOORS
St. Gregory the Martyr
St. Simon Stock
St. Nicholas

FOURTH STATION OF THE CROSS
St. Ignatius Loyola
St. Basil
St. Elizabeth Seton

CONFESSIONAL
St. Benedict
St. Dominic
St. John of the Cross

FIFTH STATION OF THE CROSS
St. Isabella
St. Mary Magdelene
St. Agnes

O'BRIEN MEMORIAL ALTAR
St. Martin of Porres
St. Donat
St. Gerald Majella

SIXTH STATION OF THE CROSS
St. John Fisher
St. Francis de Paul
St. Benedict Joslbr

CONFESSIONAL PENITENTS' CORNER
St. Francis Xavier
St. Catherine
St. Phillip Neri
St. Margaret Bourgeoys
St. Charles Garnier
St. Antoine Daniel

St. Noel Chabanel
Sts. Jean de la Lande and René Goupil
St. Gabriel Lalemant
St. Isaac Jogues
St. Jean de Brébeuf
St. Gertrude

ON THE WALLS OF THE LEFT BELL TOWER
St. Blaise
St. Barbara
St. Aloysius
St. Ursula
St. Rose Ulin
St. Albanasius
St. Peregrine
St. Stanislaus
St. Martin
St. Paul of the Cross
St. Christina
St. Maurice

ON THE WALLS OF THE LEFT BELL TOWER
St. Edward
St. Boniface
St. Elizabeth of Hungary
St. Bruno

[BLANK]
St. Alexander
St. Clothide
St. Ferdinand
St. Denis Arpgt
St. Scholastica
St. Gilbert
St. Genevieve
St. Louis of France
St. Charles Bri
St. Theresa

CONFESSIONAL
St. Vincent de Paul
St. Jean Baptiste de La Salle
Bl. Brother André

NINTH STATION OF THE CROSS
St. Dismas
St. Alphonsus
St. Catherine Mrt.

ST. JOSEPH'S ALTAR
St. Cecilia
St. Agathe
St. Roch

TENTH STATION OF THE CROSS
Bl. Kateri Tekakwitha
St. Anthony of Padua
St. Bernard

CONFESSIONAL
St. Francis of Assisi
St. Thomas
St. John Ghiston

ELEVENTH STATION OF THE CROSS
St. Ignatius
St. Winifred
St. Thomas More

EAST DOORS
St. Oliver Plunkett
St. Margaret of Scotland
St. Palladris

TWELFTH STATION OF THE CROSS
St. Eugene
St. Celsus
St. Malaghy

CONFESSIONAL
St. Bridget
St. Helen
St. Anthony

THIRTEENTH STATION OF THE CROSS
St. Clare
St. Ambroise
St. Gregory the Great
St. Rita

BURKE MEMORIAL ALTAR
St. Marie Rose
St. Timothy
St. Stephen
St. Mark

FOURTEENTH STATION OF THE CROSS
St. Jude
St. Matthew
St. Phillip

RECONCILIATION ROOM
St. Paul
St. John the Baptist
St. Michael
St. Joachim
St. Joseph

Appendix Three

The names of those of the 199th Battalion Irish Canadian Rangers who died are inscribed on the wall of honour on either side of the O'Brien memorial altar.

SAINT PATRICK'S WORLD WAR I HONOUR ROLL

Lt.-Col Vincent O'Donahoe, Capt. Victor Holmes, Capt. Thomas, Edmund Morrison, Capt. Fred Shaughnessy, Capt. John P. Walsh, Lieut. Gerald S. Fogarty, Lieut. Basil Hingston, Lieut. Joseph J. Kavanaugh, Lieut. T. Sargent Owens, Lieut. Mario De Paul, Lieut. Basil Watson, Sgt. Michael Beaudette, Sgt. Adelbert J. Borden, Sgt. Thomas Collins, Sgt. Percy Edward Coté, Sgt. W. J. Foster, Sgt. Major James Hennessy, Sgt. Michael Hubbard, Sgt. Raymond Kearns, Sgt. Phillip Martin, Sgt. Lauchlin McDonald, Sgt. Ernest Moxham, Sgt. Harold O'Shaughnessy, Sgt. Fred George Wilshire, Corp. William Beaudette, Corp. Fred Blais, Corp. A. E. Borden, Corp. Frank Brophy, Corp. J. J. Campbell, Corp. William P. Costello, Corp. Thomas Dunne, Corp. Thomas Harrington, Corp. William John McCann, Lance-Corp Thomas Henry Betts, Lance-Corp. J.A. Miller, Lance Corp. Andrew McFaul, Cadet Paul Conroy, Gnr. James Hines Boylan, Gnr. Lincoln Carr, Gnr. P. Murray, Gnr. William J.C. O'Neill, Gnr. Alfred Walsh. Ptes: Christopher Byrne, Bernard Carroll, Edward John Casey, Clarence Carter, Thomas Casey, Leo Coady, Emmett Conroy, Stanley Darragh, Thomas Duffy, William Dunbar, Thomas Fagan, Howard Farley, Frank Fitzgerald, Fred Foster, Harold Fox, John Grant, John Griffin, James Griffith, Albert James Hill, Thomas H. Hill, Michael Holmes, Herbert Dillon Johnston, John Kinsella, John Lynch, Fred Leo McAnally, Alexander McDonald, Onley O'Keefe, Leo Patterson, Peter Ryan, William Ryan, Ed Smith, J.W.A. Smith, Peter Smith, Smith J. Stafford, William Cavin Sullivan, John Whittaker, Peter Wright, and James Arthur Wynne.

Appendix Four

THE BELLS AND THEIR INSCRIPTIONS

PIUS EDWARD VINCENT
Instaurare omnia in Christo
Renew Everything through Christ

PAUL GERALD JAMES
In Domino Confido
In the Lord I Place My Trust

PATRICK ANDREW CORNELIUS
Holy Father, Keep them in the name Whom Thou
hast given me, that they may be one

JOHN MARTIN THOMAS
I Have Loved O Lord The Beauty of Thy House

CHARLES GEORGE FREDERICK
Spes Messis in Semine
The Hope of the Harvest is in the Seed

OUR LADY OF THE MOST BLESSED SACRAMENT
Give Us This Day Our Daily Bread

CECELIA MARGARET MARY
Sing Ye to the Lord a New Canticle,
Let Them Praise His name in Choir

ALOYSISUS FRANCIS DE LA SALLE
Suffer the Little Children to Come Unto Me.

The Sanctus bell was removed. Today it is at Camp Kinkora.

Bibliography

BOOKS

L'Album du Séminaire de Montreal, 1902.

Berry, Rev. Gerald. *A Critical Period in St. Patrick's Parish, 1866-74*, The annual report of the Canadian Catholic Historical Association, 1943-1944.

Black, Conrad. *Duplessis*, McClelland & Stewart, 1976.

Bliss, Michael. *Plague: The Story of Smallpox in Montreal*, HarperCollins, 1991.

Buckley, Rev. M.B. *Diary of a Tour in America*, Sealy, Bryers & Walker, Dublin, 1886.

Cahill, Thomas. *How the Irish Saved Civilization*, Anchor Books, 1993.

Curran J.J. *Golden Jubilee of the Reverend Fathers Dowd and Toupin*, Montréal, 1877

Drouin, Clémentine, S.G.M. "Love Spans the Centuries," Vol. 2, Méridien, 1988.

Gauthier, Raymond. *Construire une église au Québec: L'Architecture religieuse avant 1939*, Libre Expression, 1994.

Hudon, Michel. *Architectural Invoice: Église St. Patrick*, (Code 4230-06-96) Gouv. du Québec, Direction du Patrimoine, 1978

Deville, Raymond. *Les Prêtres de Saint-Sulpice au Canada: Grandes figures de leur histoire*. Les Presses de l'Université Laval, 1992.

Kennedy, Janice. "Love of the Irish," *Ottawa Citizen*, March 16. 1997.

Laxton, Edward. *Famine Ships: The Irish Exodus to America, 1846-51*, Bloomsbury, 1996

Lipscombe, Robert. *The Story of Old St. Patrick's*, Montreal, 1967.

Loye, John. "Career of Father Dowd Recalled," *Montreal Gazette*, Dec. 19 and 20, 1941.

Maurault, Olivier. *Marges d'Histoire*, 1929.

Maureault, Olivier. *La Congegation Irlandaise de Montréal*, 1934, Sulpician archives.

Maguire, John Francis, MP. *The Irish in America*, Sadlier & Co., 1887.

Moore, Brian. "The Church with the Heart of Gold." *Montreal Scene*

Magazine, March 18, 1974.

Noppen, Luc. *Les Chemins de la Memoire*, Région de Montréal, Tome II.

O'Gallagher, Marianna. *St. Patrick's, Québec*, Carraig Books, 1981.

Pinard, Guy. *Montréal, Son Histoire, Son Architecture*, Tome 4, Méridien, 1991.

Quiblier, Joseph Vincent. *Notice sur le Séminaire de Montreal*, 1848. Archives of the Compagnie de Saint-Sulpice MSS 1208.

Raudsepp, Karl J. *Organs of Montreal*, Orel Press, 1993.

Smith, Gustav. *Le Guide de l'Organiste practicien*.

Slattery, T.P. *They've Got to Find Me Guilty Yet*, Doubleday Canada, 1972.

Toker, Franklin. *The Church of Notre Dame in Montreal*, McGill Queen's University Press, 1970.

True Witness and Catholic Chronicle

Wallace, Martin. *Celtic Saints*, Chronicle Books, 1995.

PAMPHLETS

St. Patrick's Church, Montreal: A Story of Seventy-Five Years. Gazette, 1922.

St. Patrick's Messenger. The monthly bulletin published between 1916 and 1964.

The Narrative of the Eucharistic Congress, September 7-11 1910. *Montreal Tribune.*

The Case of St. Patrick's Congregation as to the erection of the New Cannonical Parish of St. Patrick's. Montreal, 1866;

Objections and Remonstrances against the Dismemberement of the Ancient Parish of Montreal. Montreal, 1867